Als smile went around the world
He had a way about him that made everyone feel good about themselves
His favorite saying was Ime counting my luck stars

THE LEGEND OF
BIG BOY
Safe or Stranded

An Account of a Real Life Living Legend

JIM STONE

BALBOA.PRESS

A DIVISION OF HAY HOUSE

Balboa Press books may be ordered through booksellers or by contacting:

Balboa Press
A Division of Hay House
1663 Liberty Drive
Bloomington, IN 47403
www.balboapress.com
844-682-1282

Print information available on the last page.

ISBN: 978-1-9822-6038-5 (sc)
ISBN: 978-1-9822-6039-2 (e)

Balboa Press rev. date: 01/07/2021

Dedicated to the memory of Allen Warner

Contents

Dedication

I'm sitting in a beautiful outdoor place right now, ready to begin the telling of a true life experience that I dedicate to the memory of one of my very best friends, Allen Warner. Allen (Al) recently passed away, and will be greatly missed by me, and by many others whose lives he touched. He was a wonderful man, father, outdoors man, and my wonderful friend.

Chapter 1

A few weeks before my dear friend Al passed away, he called me on my cell phone and asked if I'd come up to his house, stating that he had something for me that might help me with my writing.

So, off to Al's house I drove. When I arrived at Al's home, he greeted me outside at the end of his driveway. There he stood with a very proud, but mischievous smile pasted on his face. As I looked at my friend, I wondered, what is he up to?

I was soon to find out that Al had a plan to help me to fulfill my dreams of writing books. Books he believed that I needed to write in order to share my experiences and to entertain the minds of the young and the old. Allowing them to be transported into my world full of adventures, stories of fun, and true stories that would come to life through my writing.

My friend Al knew me well, he knew that my mind was clear, and at peace with the world when I was in the outdoors; Whether fishing or hunting with my dogs Spruce and Oak, or just enjoying the peace and serenity of being outdoors.

I got out of my truck, and headed towards Al. The smile on his face growing and lighting up his face, his excitement apparent as he shifted from foot to foot like a cat walking on hot asphalt. "Come on, come on" he urged as he led me out behind his home to a small storage shed. The door to this shed was standing open, and I could see that the shed was full of all types of treasures. Treasures that I imagine my friend had gathered during the course of his life. Al's 'treasures' might be considered junk to some, or to most people. But to Al, they all had a special place in his mind, tangible objects that were linked to his dreams, plans, or to old memories. Each object holding reminders for him of unfulfilled dreams, or thoughts of new memories that had yet to be fulfilled.

Al pointed towards an old desk and asked me what I thought of it. I had no idea at this time the extent that Al was helping me to follow my dreams of being an author. Neither of us fully knowing just how much impact having this desk was going to be. At the time, it was just a dream in my friends mind that I would carry this desk to many different and beautiful places where my memories and my thoughts could be transferred onto paper through a pencil or pen. My friends mind somehow showing him a vivid full color dream of a simple piece of paper on the top of this old desk turning into a story, then into a book to share with the world.

I had told Al my recounting of my experience with a big dog that had been stranded high up in the mountains while protecting some very special friends of his. Friends that this big dog never gave up on protecting, encouraging, refusing to give up no matter the obstacles. I've come to realize that my friend Al was just like this dog. Even the obstacle of death has not stopped him from having an influence in my life.

My heart is broken right now with the passing of my friend Al. But as I sit here, I realize that my heart is mending, being pieced back together by recalling my fond memories of Al, and with feeling the love that is radiating through this desk that Al knew would help me to follow my dreams. He just knew that it would.

As I carry this little red desk to a serene location, my dogs at my side, my pen meets the paper as I follow my dream and begin to write a book to share with the world, the story of Big Boy. This book is for you Al, my 'thank you' for your gift of this desk that I sit here and write upon. My 'thank you' for you always believing in me, and encouraging me to follow my dreams.

Chapter 2

This story is about true friends who stick by each other through thick and thin until the very end. Always believing in each other with an unconditional love that will never fall apart or fail.

I've been thinking, yearning, and wanting to share this true story for many years. The experience is clear in my mind like it just happened yesterday.

It's a late fall day in Northern Utah. Most all of the bushes, flowers and trees are showing their last brilliant colors before being covered with snow. Mother nature has created an almost magical scene full of color that is thousands of different shades, shapes, sizes and colors. God is a master artist. Have you ever noticed that His colors in nature can never truly be reproduced by any brush or photograph? Have you ever thought about the fact that throughout the fall season, the plants and trees are getting ready to go into a deep sleep, a temporary death during the cold of winter? How beautiful this time before their death is! I can't help but wonder if this is God's hint to us that our inevitable death is really a beautiful thing. A hint of the beauty that is awaiting us after our death.

My dogs and I were out taking pictures of this fall beauty. We live in a very small town that is settled next to a lake named Bear Lake, also known as the Caribbean of the West because of the brilliant blue color of the water. It's one of the biggest natural lakes anywhere in the Western Unites States. Bear Lake is settled in a high mountain valley about 6000 feet in elevation. It's full of fish, including four of them that are not found anywhere else in the world except Bear Lake.

It's truly a beautiful place to call home. Although it does have its negative aspects. The closest town to do our shopping is about 50 miles away. You have to drive over a big mountain range full of wild, untouched country that's truly wilderness just to get to the closest Walmart.

I begin the journey, but just can't stop myself from stopping in the foothills to take some pictures. As I take pictures, my thoughts are wandering through the things that I need to get done today. My plan is, after taking pictures to try to capture this magnificent beauty, my dogs and I will continue to head over to the city to pick up some supplies for the coming winter months that would be upon us very soon.

Going to the city and shopping are not even close to the top of my list of favorite things to do. But after taking some pictures, I tell my dogs that it's time we just get the shopping over and done with. We had just come up over the summit and were heading through an area full of jagged steep mountains, small box canyons, steep inclines and cliffs. The type of cliffs that if you get stranded on one of them, you might never be rescued or even found. This is the kind of country that if you didn't have a rope and climbing gear, then it's not a good idea to mess with it except with your camera.

I can never make this drive without noticing how beautiful this country is. I was driving the speed limit at 55mph when I noticed a white flash high up on the steep mountain side. I slowed down to have another look. You know, like a double take. There was nothing there. My dogs saw it to, they perked up and my dog Spruce let out a couple of 'woof woof's' like he does when he sees another dog. Spruce thinks that he is a tough dog. He is a chocolate Labrador. My other dog's name is Oak. He is a big lover boy.

I pulled off to the side of the road, and came to a complete stop. I placed the truck in park and shut off the engine. I got out my binoculars and started searching the mountain side to try to spot that white flash that we all thought we had seen. I scanned the whole mountain, spotting some deer, 2 bull elk, a few hawks, magpies and crows. Nothing white, what I saw was mostly sheer cliffs and mountain ash.

Mountain ash is a bush that produces a bright orange cluster of berries that remind me of a cluster of grapes except only about a quarter of grape size. They're really not a very good berry for human consumption. But, they are a delicacy for the birds, they are especially a favorite of the wild grouse. In these mountain forests there are blue grouse and ruffled grouse. The grouse dine on ash berries from mid-September into the middle of winter if not covered by the snow. The berries are a life line food source for all kinds of wild mountain birds. Birds are about the only animals able to reach many of the berries as the berries grow mostly on the steep mountainsides. Mountain ash is a unique plant that is able to thrive with little water, and is able to produce a bountiful harvest.

We love to hunt and harvest grouse. They are about the size of a barn yard chicken except they don't taste like chicken at all. Their meat is dark and rich with a sweet berry flavor and is very lean with hardly any fat. The blue grouse are the bigger of the 2 birds. The blue grouse are kind of like the king of the forest. When they jump up to take flight, they sound like a helicopter taking off. They have very powerful wings and can take off and fly straight up in the air again just like a helicopter.

Well, I guess that I should get back to the story. The dogs and I decided that that maybe we didn't see anything. Hey, maybe we had caught a glimpse of the elusive Sasquatch? HeHeHe. Seeing nothing out of the ordinary, I started up the truck and we pulled back out onto the road and continued on our way.

I just couldn't help myself from stopping in the lower canyon to pull out the fly rod to see if I could catch some fresh wild trout for dinner. I love fresh trout with wild gooseberry currants cooked right along with the trout. If you like capers on your fish, then you'd like currants as they are similar. Currants have a citrus flavor almost like squeezing a lemon over your fish, they kind of just go hand in hand. This time of the year, the currants were perfect for picking. I used to pick the currants before fishing, but it seemed to jinx our fishing success by having berries and then catching no fish. So now, I make sure that I catch some wild trout before picking the wild currants on the way home. On this day I was blessed to catch 6 nice wild cutthroat trout.

After cleaning the fish and putting them on ice in the cooler, we continued our drive into town. I made a quick run through the store, getting the needed supplies. I'm not a big fan of being in the city, so I normally get what I need in a big hurry and get out of Dodge fast, heading back to the mountain country. On our way back over the mountain, I need to stop to pick the wild gooseberry currants to go with my fish dinner. We stopped and hiked into one of my favorite gooseberry patches. The dogs had a fun time exploring and doing their 'business' while I picked about 3 cups of the currants. It was going to be a 5 star supper for all of us.

It was a good hike to get back to where I had parked the truck. There was so much beauty around that we kept getting side tracked taking pictures and just admiring all the beauty surrounding us. Besides all the beauty, the biggest side track was that the wild huckleberries were ripe for the picking. So of course I couldn't pass up getting a handful of yummy sweet goodness. For some reason, if the huckleberries were ripe, no berries would be left behind. Sitting under a huckleberry bush in the beautiful mountain with all of the clean fresh air is better than watching a movie while eating popcorn. One handful leads to another, then another, another, may be just one or two more handfuls until before I know it, the bushes are all bare. Huckleberries don't have butter and salt like popcorn, but they are very tasty. They explode in your mouth with a sweet berry blast of juice.

The last huckleberry bush had been raided, my hands, tongue and lips, even my t shirt were all bright purple from the wild huckleberry snack. I felt like I was getting away with eating desert before dinner instead of after dinner. Well heck, I don't have anyone to answer to but my 2 dogs and they don't care. After getting their opinion on the subject, we decided that may be that's how it should be. Who was it anyway that made the rule that desert should wait until the main course is finished?

We made it back to the truck, the dogs loaded up, Spruce winning the race into the front seat. Oak proved that he didn't really mind as he laid down and stretched out across the full length of the back seat in the crew cab truck. After placing the gooseberry currants into the cooler, I made my best attempt to wash the purple juice off of my face and hands. The stains left on my t shirt will be another story. Succeeding in at least removing the stickiness, I get behind the wheel and we are off, heading back over the high mountain range back to Bear Lake to enjoy the bounty of our harvest of wild trout and wild gooseberry currants.

The sunshine was reflecting intensely in my rear and side view mirrors as we headed up the mountain. May be it was due to all the sugar in the huckleberries, for some reason my thoughts were giddy and I started thinking about 'Mister Sun.' Isn't there a song about Mister Sun? HeHeHe. Mister Sun was nearing the end of his day of spreading sunshine in this part of the world. His job of heating and nourishing all living things in mother natures playground was coming to a close. Mister sunshine's job is never truly ever done, there are no days off for him. He does his job in one part of the world, and then just moves on to continue his unending job in another part. He's a hard worker, never being able to go on vacation or even just chill out, kicking off his shoes, taking a break while sipping on a cool drink. I'd have to say that Mister Sun is one of the hardest workers in the whole world. I wonder when he applied for this position if he knew what he was getting himself into. He's had the same job for thousands and thousands of years, never getting any time off. He's dedicated as they come. He must love his job. Anyway, Mister sun is about ready for his shift change. Then it's going to start to get dark pretty quickly.

My pondering about Mister Sun helped to pass several miles and now we were almost back to where earlier we had thought that we had seen a white flash on the steep cliffs high up on the mountain. I slowed down to about half of the speed limit to get a good glance at the wild steep mountainside, passing through the area with no sighting of a flash of white.

Chapter 3

I had driven a couple miles further up the steep canyon road when we came upon a huge pure white dog. I slowed the truck way down and was following behind the dog. The dog was zigzagging back and forth with his nose to the ground. It appeared to me that the dog was heading somewhere. It was a male dog, he was huge with fluffy white fur. He wasn't walking or running, but prancing like one of those pure bred horses that knows he is going to win the blue ribbon in a competition. How picture perfect this dog was. He looked like he was a middle aged dog, not young but a long ways from old.

As we followed behind the dog, watching and wondering just what this dog was doing here, my instincts were telling me that this dog was looking for something, or may be someone. As we gained on the dog and passed on by, the dogs nose never left searching all the scents on the ground. He reminded me of my hunting dogs, hot on a trail, using their noses to follow a downed bird or flush a new bird out into the air for me to get a shot and chance at harvesting the game bird.

There's not too many things more beautiful than watching a hunting dog use his nose while being excited. Letting his or her instinct to hunt come to the surface. A dogs drive to do what it was bred and born to do is just simply amazing, it's what dogs do.

We got a ways out in front of this dog, and pulled over on the opposite side of the road so we didn't interfere with what ever he was looking for. While watching the dog in the rear view mirror, he turned off of the side of the road and disappeared into the forest. May be he had found what he was looking for? Or hopefully had found his owner. Since the dog was now out of sight, I pulled back onto the road and continued on.

Chapter 4

T he remainder of my drive home, I could not get this dog off of
my mind. Wondering if he had indeed found his owner? I got to
thinking that there were no roads in the area where the dog had
gone off of the road. Since I didn't know for sure, I began worrying
about the dog. If the dog was up there alone, I couldn't figure out what
that big dog was doing so far up in the mountains this time of year.
Great Pyrenees are used by ranchers in the area to guard sheep, but
it was too late in the season for sheep to be ranging on the National
Forest. Most government agencies have rules and regulations set forth
to stop all grazing on public, state and federal lands about mid to end
of September.

I'm thinking that the cattle and sheep seem to know that when the
nights get long and cold, it's time to head off the mountain. It could be
an instinct embedded in their genes from the time when they were all
wild, or a learned behavior. Whether instinct or a learned habit of the
elders, something triggers all of them to follow trails to roads, the roads
leading them all back to the safety of their home. But occasionally stock
does get lost, or young calves and lambs do get separated. There could
be any number of reasons for stock to still be up on the mountain. Many
modern day ranchers that use mountains for grazing in the summers are
implanting GPS tracking chips in some or all of their stock and their
dogs. Doing this helps the ranchers keep tract of their animals, and are
able to locate them easily should they need to be moved during the
season, or to locate them at the seasons end. Doing this also helps if for
some reason the stock or a dog does get separated, lost or stranded due
to an early or unexpected storm.

My mind is reeling with worry for this dog as I pull into my driveway. We are home safe. We have made our way home basically doing what all Gods creatures do to keep fed, safe and warm.

Us humans have it so much easier than animals, especially the wild animals. Us humans go shopping just as I had done today. We can catch wild fish or hunt wild game and pick wild berries. We store our supplies in our homes just as a squirrel stores his winter supplies. Difference is that us humans purchase our supplies with ease, if we don't have a successful hunt or if we don't catch any fish it's no big deal. We have ample supplies and we can just open up our fridge, turn on the stove and pour us a cold drink while supper cooks. Having most everything we need right in our homes.

Can you imagine being hungry with no food in your home, not having any grocery stores available like we have? Where we can jump in our cars, travel 65 miles an hour and be where we can get supplies of what ever we need in just a few minutes. Filling our shopping carts to the brim with anything we want. It's such a luxury that God's creatures in wild places just don't have.

I often count my lucky stars that I'm so blessed with so many many grand blessings. I forget sometimes to take the time to consciously thank our Heavenly Father for all of these blessings. To be thankful for every single thing including all of the small things that I take for granted. Like being able to turn on the tap and have cold clean water flowing right here inside of my home, filling up my glass instead of having to hike or fly miles to even be able to get a cold drink like all animals and birds have to do. It's a small thing for all of us that is taken for granted.

Chapter 5

My mind was distracted from thoughts of the dog and all the wild creatures as I prepared my trout and currant dinner while watching an episode of Gold Prospectors on the TV. Sitting on my couch the dogs and I ate my dinner as I sat with my feet propped up. A beautiful sunset was casting a soft red glow on the walls of my living room. The birds in the trees just outside of my window are singing their final praises, thanking God for all of their blessings of the day. It's getting late, just about to get dark. My day is coming to an end. Spruce and Oak went to their beds right after I finished sharing my dinner with them. Hey guys what about the dishes? I'm stuck again with cleaning up. Dang dogs have such an easy life.

After getting everything cleaned up and put away, dishes washed and the floor swept and mopped, I shut off the TV, got my nightly hygiene done and I go to bed.

I lay here in bed unable to sleep, my eyes are wide open as my thoughts shift to that big beautiful dog all alone late in fall high up in a very desolate mountain range. Is that beautiful dog lost? He isn't stranded, he can freely follow the road. It just seemed odd, something would not allow me to let go of my worry for this dog. Everything that I saw keeps replaying in my mind. What if this dog was still protecting something or someone? Was he trying to find his way home? What was he searching for with his nose to the ground zigzagging back and forth on a busy road? It's starting to baffle my mind about this big dog seemingly all by himself. If it were me all alone in the wild mountain range, it could not only be very dangerous, but it would be really lonely. What is he doing? Why is he still up there? Does he have a home to go to? Is he homeless? Is he lost? Does he need help? Then, just like you would see in a cartoon, a light bulb came on in my mind. My mind suddenly lit up with what made the remainder of the night sleepless for me. That dog was hungry! That dog was searching for something to eat while he zigzagged on the side of the road! That's it, my question had been answered. That dog needed my help, he was hungry, in my mind he needed food.

It was now set in my mind that the dog was searching for food. That dog is hungry. I've got to do something even if my thoughts are wrong. I've got to try. I'm going to take some food up there as soon as this long sleepless night passes by. Mister sunshine gets up at the crack of dawn and I'm getting up with him! As soon as morning gets here, I'm heading up into the mountains to find that dog and take him some food.

I look over at my clock, it's 2:30 AM and I haven't slept a wink. Come on time, please hurry up. I need a fast forward button on the clock to make the time just fly by, misses time needs to wake up mister sunshine a little bit earlier than he wants to. Hurry up misses time, I've got things on my mind, I've got places to be and things to do. Please hurry up, I've got to help that dog fill up his belly with a good meal.

I'm watching my big bay window that faces east where I'm impatiently awaiting a small faint light revealing the peaks of the mountain range that borders the east side of the valley. When the sun comes up, it will expose a giant fresh water lake with magical shimmering colors of blue. The early morning rays of the sun casting surreal colors of orange, reds or pinks across the surface of the water.

Chapter 6

As a faint glow appears behind the east mountains, I'm up and dressed in record time.

Spruce and Oak both greet me with excited wags and are prancing around me, hopping and circling me as I gather the food to take to that big dog. It's amazing how dogs can feel their owners anticipation.

Having packed up the food for this dog inside my large backpack, out we go into the crisp fall morning. The dogs loaded up in the truck, and I placed the heavy backpack into the bed of the truck. Inside the pack I had a bag of bagels, beef bones with a generous portion of meat still on them, a bag of dog food and a big pan to put the dog food in, a water dish, and a gallon jug of water.

I'm hoping that this big dog would be close to the first place we had seen him yesterday. If we didn't see him, my plan was to still leave the food and water there. Then I'll go check on it tomorrow morning to see if it had been touched, or hopefully all eaten by that beautiful dog. It was about a 20 mile drive to get there. To get there, I'll have to go all the way up one side of the mountain, passing over the top of the summit, then 5 miles down off the other side.

I'm really really anxious and in a hurry, so I'm going to stop on my way up into the mountain, and get some of that nutritious breakfast food from the convenience store, and a couple of big beef jerky sticks for Spruce and Oak, and top off my fuel.

Whoo hoo! I'm on my way to bring food and the extra jerky treat to a dog that I haven't even met yet. A dog that I briefly encountered, and can't get off my mind. A dog that I spent a sleepless night worried about.

It's a gorgeous late fall day. Most all of the maple and aspen trees had dropped their leaves. The early morning sun is enhancing the bright fall colors of all of the remaining leaves left clinging to the trees. I can't help but admire the brilliant reds with spotty golds mixed in, the almost florescent yellows and even a little pink. All the berry bushes I'm passing still have their leaves with late season fruits still on them. My mouth waters as I think of how the wild berries get better after a few days of frost or with cold weather. They just burst with sweetness, full of juice when you pop them in your mouth. It's sheer yumminess, natures pure wild goodness. Mother nature never ceases to amaze me, that because of the sugar content, wild berries and other wild fruits including apples, resist freezing through a few days of freezing temperatures. The cold and freezing temperatures make the fruits sweeter, making them a treat to be enjoyed by wildlife and some of us humans who enjoy consuming the bounties of the wild.

We were almost to where we had spotted that white flash high up on the steep mountainside full of drastic overhanging cliffs. Just before we arrived, I noticed that an adjacent mountainside was covered with mountain ash. The berries on mountain ash are one of the wild birds' most favorite forage foods. The bushes had all their leaves that had turned bright orange to match their clumps of late fall berries. Their berries look like clusters of grapes, but are comparable in size to snap peas. It was so beautiful to see a whole mountainside of bright orange. I'm always reminded when I see the abundance of available wild food of just how amazing it is how heavenly Father has provided for his creatures. High calorie wonderful food to help sustain them through the upcoming winter months that would soon be here. A cold, harsh winter that lasts about 4 months before spring arrives.

We were here. I left my dogs safe in the truck while I put on my pack and hiked up the steep mountain. I'm hoping that my thoughts of the dog being hungry will turn out to be wasted worry. But, if the dog is still up here, I hope that he's still around this area. When I had hiked about 50 yards off the road, I placed the food and water dishes at the base of a tree where the ground was pretty level. I filled up both dishes, then I scattered in 4 different places the bagels and bones.

Cupping my hands around my mouth, I hollered in several directions; Here boy, here boy, here boy. Come on boy. Here boy, I have food for you boy. Come and get it boy. Come here boy, here boy, come and eat boy. I stood and listened each time after yelling, hearing only the wind as it meandered through the trees. My yelling seems to be failing to create any results. I sat on a boulder for several minutes just listening. The wind, a few crows, a tree squirrel cussing at me, and the screech of a hawk that was riding a high wind current were all that I heard.

Before heading back down to the truck, I decided to give a few more yells. Here boy, come on boy, here boy, come and eat boy. Then, coming from up higher on the mountain I hear 'roof, roof, roof, roof, bark, bark, woof' was it him? It had to be him! He had come back to this spot where I had first seen the flash of white! He was still here! Here boy, here boy, come get it. 'Woof, woof, woof.' He was here, just like I had wished for!

'Roof, roof, roof.' He was coming down the mountain towards me, his barks getting louder as he got closer.

'Woof, woof.' Here boy, here Boy, come on Boy. I'm elated with joy! He was here! Here boy, come get it boy. As suddenly as the barks had started, the barks had stopped, there were no more barks. Come on boy. Here boy, here boy. Only the sound of the wind in the trees. No barks. No dog.

I waited silently for several minutes. Still no dog appeared. Well, not knowing too much about Great Pyrenees behaviors, I decided it may be best if I just backed off. I hiked back down to my truck. My 2 dogs, Spruce and Oak both looking at me from inside the truck as if they were wondering, 'What is Jimmy doing? How come he is yelling "here boy, here boy, come on boy." Doesn't he know we are locked in the truck? Hey Spruce, do you think Jimmy is getting old and loosing his mind?' Hehehe hoo!

I got into the truck, rolled the window down and got my binoculars out, I began searching the mountainside for all the possible places that the dog could be up on that steep mountainside. I could see the area where I had left the food and water, but there was no movement, no sign of the dog coming to get his food. After a few more minutes I'm thinking that maybe it's best if we leave here, head back home and return tomorrow morning, checking on his food to see if he had been there having a good dinner.

We were off, heading home, my thoughts still wondering about this dog. Either he, or another dog was definitely there. If it's the same dog, why did he go back to that spot instead of continuing down the road? Or were there 2 dogs? I'm hoping that after we left, the dog traveled down to eat some, or all of the food that we had left. I'll find out when I return tomorrow morning with more food and water to hopefully refill the empty dishes and take some more treats.

Chapter 7

I t was a hard job, and it took a lot of hours to run 2 businesses plus be an outfitter. My 2 stores would be closed up soon for the winter. The stores are only open for about 5 months during the tourist season. Most all of the stores and other businesses are only open from early May until mid October. Closing their doors for the winter until the next spring.

The months that my stores are closed, the hunting seasons are open. October through January is my busy season for outfitting and guiding people from all over the world. I guide for a little bit of everything, from small game, big game, bait fishing, spin cast fishing and my most loved thing to guide, fly fishing!

Most everyday of the week, I'm up and out in the field from early morning until late at night. I'm concerned about having the time to be able to take food and water up on the mountain. By taking the food I'm hoping to not just provide the dog with the nutrition and water that he needs, but most importantly to gain this dog, or dogs trust to where I can get him safely back to his home before winter sets in.

I decided to make a couple of phone calls to local ranchers who I knew ranged their sheep up in the mountains on the National Forest during the summer. I made some calls, but came up with nothing. None of the ranchers said that they were missing a Great Pyrenees.

Not having any success with locating a rancher that was missing a dog, I decided that it was up to me to make a commitment to this dog. To me a commitment is the same as making a promise that cannot, and will not be broken for any reason that's within my control. I'm committed to do my best to get this dog off of the mountain. Taking food and water up the mountain for as long as I need to gain this dogs trust so that I will be able to save this dogs life. I'm willing to be there for him until either he's gone, or I'm gone. A promise is a promise, I promise that I'm going to rescue this dog!

Chapter 8

Night time again seemed like an eternity, it just couldn't get light soon enough. Waiting again for the sun to get back to this part of the world and start spreading his light. Sunlight was essential to be able to see to hike up the mountain to see if the dog had been able to find his food that I had left him yesterday morning. But, I couldn't sleep and my anxiety level was high, so off we went in the dark. We stopped on our way out of town and got a cup of hot cocoa and more convenience store nutritious food; A microwave breakfast sandwich for all 4 of us. I bought a 5 pound bag of kibbles to leave whether or not it had been eaten. I suspect, but I'm still not certain that the dog I had heard barking was the same big white dog that I had seen. Whether it was that dog, or another, I'm committed to provide help. My plan this morning is to hike up as far as I can, hopefully getting the food and water closer to where the barking had come from.

We arrived and parked the truck. It's still dark, way too early to try to hike, so we're sitting here in the truck having our hot cocoa and breakfast while listening to soft music. I have the windows rolled down just in case we might hear a big loud bark. The minutes drag on and on until it's finally light enough to see to make the hike.

It's time Spruce and Oak, you guys stay here and be good boys while I go check on the dog food that we left yesterday. If I'm not back soon, don't worry because I'm going to hike a little bit further to leave some more food. I packed the bag of kibbles and the last breakfast sandwich along with a gallon jug of water into my pack and off I went.

I got to the place where I had left the dishes of water and food. All of the food was gone! Had the big dog been here? Did he eat the food that I had left? Dang, is his belly full? I sure hope so. Looking around at the ground around the dishes, I see deer and elk tracks. Would they eat bagels and dog food? Good question. I didn't think so, but who knows. Just like yesterday I cup my hands around my mouth and holler in several different directions; Here boy, here boy, come on boy, here boy come eat your food boy. Silence. Not even the wind is meandering through the trees. I holler several more times, and wait. No sounds, just the still silence of an early morning mountain. There were no barks this time. I'm feeling frustrated not being able to know for sure if the big dog had eaten his food. All of the big game tracks had me wondering who or what had eaten it. I tell myself, stay positive Jimmy, at least his food was gone.

I put the dishes in my pack, and hiked as far as I could, my ascent stopped by the overhanging cliffs. I located a semi level place that was big enough to set the dishes without the risk of them sliding down the steep mountain. I fill them both up and place the breakfast sandwich on the top of the kibbles. I'm wishing that I had a trail camera to set up by the dishes. Since I don't have one, I decide to do the next best thing that I can think of. I break off a tree branch, and use the branch like a garden rake or broom. Sweeping the top of the dirt, removing any rocks or existing tracks away to make a smooth surface that would reveal any new animal tracks in the dirt.

Having the food site all prepared, I'm ready to hike back to the truck and head out to take some clients fishing for wild brook trout in a small creek up one of Bear Lake Utah's most beautiful canyons. It would be a long day not being able to return back here to check on the dogs food until early tomorrow morning.

When I get back to my truck and start it up, the clock on the dash comes on and I see that I was longer than I thought I had been with spending time to sweep and prepare the ground to be able to identify any new animal tracks. I'm going to have to really hurry back home to meet up with my clients. I'll make it just barely I think. The extra time will hopefully pay off, and I'm hoping to see only the dogs tracks at the food dish early tomorrow morning.

Chapter 9

My clients were waiting for me when I arrived home. I was only about 15 minutes late, so it wasn't a big deal even though I apologized for my tardiness. I packed up the cooler with lunches that I had prepared yesterday evening, sandwiches, chips, snacks and drinks to take and we headed out.

We had a wonderful day fishing, catching wild brook trout on dry flies. Brook trout are an amazing fish, they have all the colors of a rainbow on them; blue, orange, red, light faded pink, white, silver and black. Brook trout are a mixture of a lake trout with some arctic char in them. Brook trout only live in clean, clear, freestone brooks and streams or high mountain pristine lakes.

They are one of mother natures most beautiful fish. Brook trout have a pure white stripe on the bottom of their pectoral fins. When you sneak up on a hole, or even better, a beaver dam, you really can't see the fish. What you can see are their white fins shifting from side to side as they move around underneath the crystal clear water. They make the bottom of the river or lake shimmer with streaks of pure white, creating movement and giving away the presence of life underneath the clear water.

The whole time that I was fishing, I had that big dog on my mind. Just hoping that he had been been what had eaten the food yesterday, and praying that he was eating it again after I left it early this morning.

Chapter 10

Again I got up early with mister sunshine. Us dogs were making getting up early a habit. It was a good habit to be in as we have been blessed to see every sunrise for the last 3 days straight. None of them were the same, they all were beautiful in their own way, so different from each other.

I used to guide this man for water foul hunting, his most favorite thing to do was to be out sitting on a beautiful marsh while it was still pitch black dark. It touches your soul to be out there listening to all of Gods creatures that live there. Hearing them as they all sing their different songs of praise to God, being grateful for a new day.

This man's favorite saying was; 'Did you know Jimmy that if you miss a day in the great outdoors, you've lost out. A day missed sitting here in this place is a unique day that doesn't come twice.' This man is passed away now, but his favorite saying still sticks in my mind. So to me, this habit of getting up early to go feed this dog has been a good thing. I've been seeing things that I might not ever see again. It makes my friend that's gone come forth, back to life in my memories of our time spent with each other seeing wild things that we will never see again.

We've made the familiar drive and are here on the mountain again, bringing more food and water. I'm ready for another hike, anxious to find out if there are dog tracks and if the food is gone. You dogs stay here, I'll be right back. As I hiked up to where I had left the food yesterday morning, my mind was making a wish that there would be an empty food dish with that dogs footprints all around where I had swept the soil free of all tracks. I had the remainder of the bag of kibbles and about half of a pound of leftover venison roast from a few nights ago. I thought that some fresh meat would be a yummy treat for this dog if he would just please show up. Please Mr. Dog let me help you get to a safe place before winter, hopefully to your home where you'll be safe. This is no place for you to be with a cold freezing winter that is coming very soon.

My jaw dropped wide open when I saw that the dog food was gone, with no other prints around the dishes except very large dog prints. Now I knew for sure that a dog was eating the food. Whether it was the big white dog that I had seen on the road, I still didn't know for sure. But I was happy to be able to verify that a dog had eaten the food, and I just knew that it was that big beautiful white Pyrenees dog. My heart was filled with joy! He's been here! He's been here! He has a full belly! That big dog was here! My efforts are not in vain!

I refilled his dishes with food and fresh water, placing the left over roast on top of the kibble. Where, oh where, is this big dog? And why is he still here so high up in this huge mountain range? Why won't he come down? What is this big dog doing? Doesn't he want to get out of here? Heading for his home where he has food, warmth and some companionship? I spend a lot of time by myself, but after so long by myself, I start yearning for someone to talk to, and I enjoy having the comforts at my home.

I holler and holler for the dog, but like the day before there are no answering barks. I'm just going to have to take comfort knowing that the dog is coming to the food and water. I've got to somehow get the dog close enough so that he can get used to me and trust me if I'm going to be successful in getting him off of this mountain before the snow flies.

I yelled a few more times for this big dog, but he wouldn't answer. My plan was to come fill his dish as close to this same time everyday as possible, hoping that it would become his habit also to come get his food at this time everyday. It's going to take some time to earn this dogs trust. I just have to keep coming everyday.

Well, it was time for me to hit the trail back to the truck. I had to take some more fishermen out. Today I'm taking my clients out on Bear Lake to fish for the giant native Bonneville cutthroat trout. Bear Lake boasts some of the biggest wild trout in all the world. Some of these trout would exceed 20 pounds. They take on a sky blue color on their backs almost identical to the sky blue color from Bear Lakes clear Caribbean blue water. The deposits of calcium carbonate from sandstone that penetrate Bear Lake's water is what causes it to turn blue. The blue coloring is transferred to the cutthroat trout, giving them a unique, beautiful blue coloring on their backs. They are a rare trout, mostly found in Utah and Idaho with a few in Wyoming. Their blue color with the bright orange on their cheeks, and a mixture of scarlet reds mixed with orange on the underside of their gills like a stripe coming out of their jaws underneath their mouth makes them a favorite to catch. Fisherman come from all over to get a chance to catch one of these rare impressive beauties. Today, my fishing clients had traveled from back east to hopefully catch some of these rare cutthroat trout.

Chapter 11

In order to fulfill my desire to earn this dogs trust, I had been doing a lot of research on Great Pyrenees dogs. To a lot of ranchers, they are just a working dog. From birth they have no human contact. They are raised with livestock, learning from their parents to guard and to fight to the death protecting all of the animals under their watch even though Great Pyrenees are also known to be very gentle and full of love for humans. They are a big hearted dog that craves attention. They are kind of like a work horse of sorts to some people, but to other people they are a loving companion or best friend for life.

Great Pyrenees are a large breed of dog that are bred to protect livestock. They are like guardian angels. They will ward off any threatening predators like bears, mountain lions, wolves, and the coyotes that we have in this part of the country. Great Pyrenees will fight to the death of themselves or whatever they are fighting against.

Great Pyrenees are a huge dog with a great big heart to match their size. Great Pyrenees were originally from France and Spain. Great Pyrenees arrived in the Pyrenean mountains with their shepherds around the year 3,000 BC. The experts opinion think that the Great Pyrenees breed evolved from white mountain dogs that originated in Asia from a time 11,000 years ago. Great Pyrenees were bred to be nocturnal so that they could guard the flock in the middle of the night while us humans got some sleep. Great Pyrenees like to bark and bay in the middle of the night to deter predators from getting too comfortable in trying to attack and harm any of the animals that the Great Pyrenees are protecting. Great Pyrenees make good pets for company and companions to humans. They are very affectionate and loving but at the same time are ferocious, protecting all of us from harms way. Great Pyrenees are instinctively nurturing. For thousands of years the Great Pyrenees was a dog for peasants who were livestock farmers. Then he gained nobility in the renaissance years. They were known as the great dogs of the mountains. They were soon the protectors of Lords, Kings and royalty.

At one time King Louis XIV's court had declared the Great Pyrenees the royal dog of France. Queens and Kings loved the breed. At one time even Queen Victoria owned one to protect her and watch over her well being.

The Great Pyrenees was brought to the United States by the Marquis De Lafayette. He was a French military officer who was fighting in the American Revolutionary war. The Marquis brought a pair of Great Pyrenees to the United States in 1842 as a gift to one of his friends.

The Great Pyrenees breed was used in WWII as a standard guard dog. They were also used as pack animals, bringing supplies and artillery over the Pyrenees mountains. They are very large dogs, some exceeding over 160 pounds. They are gentle giants until someone or something threatens their friends, then they become an unstoppable force full of rage which is seldom matched by anything.

Great Pyrenees are pretty common in the western United States. We see a lot of them in Bear Lake Utah. Normally they are on the borders of their flocks of sheep, scanning the area for any threatening predators planning on getting an easy meal. Boy do the predators get a big surprise when they try to get that easy meal. Normally ranchers will always have more than one Great Pyrenees depending on the size of their flock of sheep. They are such smart dogs. When small groups of sheep go astray from the big group, a Pyrenees will break off of the group leaving other Pyrenees behind to look after the remainder of the flock. The single dog watches after the small group until they are safely back with the larger group.

Chapter 12

We had a super fishing trip on Bear Lake Utah. Some fish we landed were over 10 pounds. I always do a little schooling to my clients before we embark on any outdoors trip. One thing that I always try to teach them is to properly handle a wild fish, that unless we are going to harvest that fish it needs to be treated gentle. Hopefully never being lifted from it's home in the fresh clear cold water. Also never being touched with dry or oily hands. If it's hooked in a manner where the hook is too deep, we just clip the line as close to the hook as possible. This allows mister or misses fish to return to their home in good health. Most all hook companies are required to develop hooks to dissipate or erode within just a few weeks, falling from a fish without harming them. Some people who want to have a big fish mounted for a trophy or display in their homes don't have to take the actual fish. We just measure it's length and girth then take pictures of all it's amazing colors and features. Then send this information to a taxidermist who artistically recreates an identical fish mount. Still being able to let the real fish return to live another day. It's really neat how you can hold onto such a grand memory, mounting your fish but not having to do any harm to such a beautiful creature.

After the long successful day of fishing, night time was here. I felt like I might be able to get a little sleep tonight, unlike previous nights. It was comforting just thinking that big dog had a full belly and that he was probably sleeping better also.

Morning came soon, so off we went to refill our new friends dish with all kinds of yummy things for him to nourish his massive body. Giving him strength to do whatever he was doing so high up in these mountains.

I parked and practiced my same habit of cracking open my truck windows and locking it up to keep Oak and Spruce safe, then off I went on my hike, hoping not only did that big dog eat his food, but maybe he was still there, maybe he just might come to me today. He's got to know that it's me that's been feeding him, not doing him any harm, in fact just the opposite; I'm trying to rescue him.

I'm almost to where his food dish was when there he was, sitting like a sculpture about 100 yards up on the side of a very steep hill of cliffs on the mountainside. His ears were perked up, the only movement was his big brown eyes following my every footstep or movement. Not wanting to alarm him, I proceeded to his food dish, filling it up full of kibbles topped with some fresh meat with rice and cooked fresh vegetables. It was a meal fit for a king exactly like this big dog is. He's king of this big mountain. As I looked his way, he sat still as if he were posing to have his picture painted into an oil painting or life sized portrait painted by a world famous artist. A priceless gift to hang on a museum wall, being admired by all who passed by awestruck at viewing such a monarch of such a wild place.

It was important to not alarm this dog. I wanted not only to gain his trust, but I really wanted him to see me and to smell my scent so that he could be ensured that I was no threat to him. After filling his food, I decided maybe it was best to just turn around, leaving him alone for today. While hiking back to my truck, where my dogs are patiently awaiting my arrival my heart becomes so full of such a true love with a close second feeling of satisfaction. It was one of those feelings that is almost overwhelming. Just a really fulfilling feeling. It made me think of all of our dogs. Our dogs love us with all of their hearts as we love them with all of our hearts. Speaking for myself, there's not a better friend, nor is there better company than a dog.

Driving back home, my thoughts go back to when I was a young man, I had the good fortune to be a hunting and fishing guide in Alaska. I had a dog named Bozwood that was my companion throughout my time guiding there. Bozwood was a big dog, he never left my side. He was my protector and my companion that was more than a best friend. Bozwood was fearless, he would fend off wolves, bears and even bad people that he just seemed to know were up to no good. Our dogs seem to have a sixth sense in addition to their nose that can sniff out arriving trouble way before it gets here. For me, Bozwood was an angel come to life, sent into this world to be my true friend. Guarding me until death did we part. I'm reminded of my dog Bozwood when I think of this big dog running wild up here, my thoughts were that this big dog was doing exactly what Bozwood had done for me. For 16 years Bozwood stayed by my side as we shared so many adventures that I may have to write another book to tell his story.

Chapter 13

Every time I thought about this big dog, I wondered what his name was. Or if he even had a name. When I next call to him, I'd like to call him by a name, a fitting, appropriate name. 'Here boy' wasn't going to cut it. So my thoughts were, well, he's a boy dog, also a big dog. I've got it, I've got his name! His name would be 'Big Boy.' Yep, I like his new name, Big Boy suited him just fine. I'm hoping that Big Boy would like it and answer to his new name. Next time our eyes meet while I'm hiking in to fill his food dish, it would be time to greet him calling his new name. Here Big Boy, here Big Boy.

Yep, he was now known as Big Boy. It's a fitting name for such a big beautiful mountain dog.

For the next couple of weeks, I continue to make the daily drive, and make my trek up to deliver food, water and of course treats for this big dog. Each day he is just a little bit further down, closer to where the dishes are, he is getting used to me and is counting on me to be here at about the same time everyday. Everyday I call him by his name, Big Boy. I don't linger, I've been placing the food and water and heading back to my truck.

My next trip up the mountain with Big Boy's supplies, I plan on staying for awhile. I think that I can coax him down. It's time to meet Big Boy in person. Face to face, voice to voice, eye to eye. Being really nervous to meet Big Boy, my mind was pondering how he might react to meeting me. Wintertime was approaching fast. Any day now winter conditions could put an abrupt halt to this rescue mission. The time is now to push this to a new level. A level of trusting each other, a knowing from deep within that everything is going to be okay. Just knowing after this is all over, our friendship is set in stone, lasting both of our lives. Both finally getting home safe.

Chapter 14

Big Boy was on my mind throughout the night. My mind was racing 100 miles per hour, question after question with very few answers. One thing I just couldn't understand was how could someone just give up or abandon such a beautiful, majestic creature as Big Boy.

I had an idea who Big Boy belonged to. The better part of my life had been spent in the Bear Lake Valley, guiding hunters and fishermen, exploring every road and back road. Some roads that weren't even roads nor even designated trails.

I came up with the idea that I'd go early that next morning, putting off trying to meet face to face with Big Boy. I'd feed him, then I'd go to every sheep ranch in or near Bear Lake valley that may own Great Pyrenees.

There was one particular ranch that stood out in my mind. Over the last several years, I had hunted Canadian geese in the grain fields that are adjacent to this ranch. For many years when I had my dogs with me hunting, there were 5 Great Pyrenees dogs who wouldn't interfere with us or my dogs, but they would stand on the outskirts of their flock of sheep while watching our every move. Insuring that they were doing what they had been bred for, which was protecting or fending off any threats to their woolly friends. I often zoomed in on these Great Pyrenees with my spotting scope. Admiring their size with a beauty unique to them that is pretty unmatched in the dog world. Their eyes were all business at all times. Very rarely missing anything which might bring their powerful bodies into a vicious force to kill or be killed doing their duty of protecting their friends.

As I had watched these Great Pyrenees, getting more familiar with each one of them, one of them had always stood out. This one particular dog was at the front of my memory, giving me a strong gut feeling that Big Boy was one of those 5 dogs at that ranch.

Morning had finally come, I loaded up my dogs, deciding to drive out to this ranch. It's late September now, so I'm pretty sure that all of the livestock should be off of National Forest land, back to their winter homes where they could be fed, sheltered and safe from a long bitter cold winter which will soon be prevalent. Once our winter sets in, we can plan on it staying for about 5 months. Northern Utah gets well over 20 feet of heavy snow with freezing sub zero temperatures. Sometimes 35-40 below zero. Many of the wild animals can survive, but domestic animals don't stand a very good chance at surviving in these conditions. Those who regulate the grazing on our public lands, set dates for all livestock to be off the higher altitude grazing areas before winter sets in. Therefore, the livestock should all be settled in at their ranch homes for the winter, and there should be 5 Great Pyrenees with them back at this ranch where the livestock and dogs are able to shelter for wintertime.

I'm thinking that for Great Pyrenees, wintertime is like a 5 month vacation. A well needed break from a long summer of working hard 24 hours a day, 7 days a week. With no days off during the grazing season, no calling in sick, no day off to catch up on some needed rest.

We arrived at this ranch, stopping where it was okay to be without getting permission from any land owners. Knowing that Great Pyrenees will go to check on any disturbances, noises or visuals, I honked my horn, opened and closed my truck doors several times. Making sure to slam the doors shut, reopen and slam again both doors on my truck. After making a lot of noise to attract the attention of the dogs, I climbed into the back of my truck, then stood on top of my tool box, allowing me a birds eye view of this ranch where I was almost positive Big Boy should be right now.

Using my spotting scope, I scanned over the herd of sheep spread out across the field. There were only 4 dogs that I could see, all 4 of them running towards my truck to investigate the loud ruckus that I had made on purpose to draw out the beautiful protectors of these sheep. They all stopped and stood between the flock and my truck doing their job of protecting their friends.

I climbed out of the bed of my truck and made more noise, again opening and closing doors and honking the horn. I even yelled a few times, no additional dogs appeared, there was no 5th Great Pyrenees. There only being 4 dogs could have meant many things, but in my mind it meant that this was Big Boys home, where he belonged on his winter vacation with his 4 comrades. Taking it easy, eating well, putting on weight, storing energy for the next years grazing season when all 5 of them would start their work again.

We had spend enough time here, it was time to go around and visit with all of the ranchers, trying to get information. Without being accusing, I decided to ask friendly questions like how they were doing, how was their year, how their families and health were, just basic things while trying to discover if maybe one of their Great Pyrenees wasn't accounted for yet. I didn't want to start trouble, or blame anyone, mostly I just wanted to help Big Boy get home safe. I just wanted to reach out asking for some help from anyone that might know Big Boy and where his forever home was. Big Boy is such a beautiful dog, if he were mine and he was missing, I'd be searching endlessly to find him. Ensuring his safety with me at home where he belongs.

There were 3 big ranches in the Bear Lake Valley that I knew of. They all used Great Pyrenees to protect their livestock. Me and my dogs spent all day talking with land owners. 2 Of them had brought up how it was a good year, their livestock including their guard dogs had all made it home safe.

I had decided to visit the ranch where I had scoped out the 4 Great Pyrenees last of all since it's the one that I suspected was Big Boy's home. I wanted to rule out any possibility that any of the other ranchers were missing a dog first. I got a funny gut feeling while talking to this last rancher. He for some reason caused me to feel really uneasy. I'm normally very trusting, but while talking with this rancher I felt there was some underlying factors that he wasn't being truthful about.

I had to just take it for what it was and not cause any trouble by accusing the rancher of leaving one of his dogs up on the mountain. I needed to just focus my attention back to how I could gain Big Boys trust enough to help him to stay fed while coming up with a rescue plan. Knowing that Great Pyrenees are trained to not trust or interact with people from the time that they are puppies, and that they form an incredible bond to their masters and to the livestock they are going to look after while protecting their well being, I knew it was going to take time to gain Big Boy's trust.

Chapter 15

It's getting to be late into the fall season, currently there is just a skiff of snow showing on some of the high mountain tops. Temperatures are in the low 60's during the day, with them dropping just above freezing by nightfall. It's such a beautiful time of the year in northern Utah. A few remaining brilliant scarlet reds, oranges with mixed in yellows and a plethora of plump wild plums and apples surrounded by late season wild choke cherries, rose hips, currants and my favorite berries of all, elderberries. Elderberries are a bright purple berry, they grow in big clumps of several hundred berries in each clump. They kinda look like a vine of grapes, except each berry is only about the size of a pea. When it becomes a little colder, the freezing temperatures cause the berries to gain their sweet flavor. After 2 or 3 light frosts the berries get a light white powder coating on them. They are a wonderful wild berry to use for jams, jellies, syrups, to eat plain or even cook right in with wild fish or any type of wild game.

Mother nature is so amazing how she simply provides for all of Heavenly Fathers creatures. She provides fresh bounties for them as well as bounties that are capable of preserving themselves, like wild berries which will remain on the bush, shrink in size when they dry, but still provide a good food source throughout the winter months for all who take the time to notice or to find them. Wild animals, mostly birds, come to depend on these resources to survive an oncoming long, harsh wintertime. In Heavenly Father's master plan of creating wildlife, He included the many food sources to provide His creatures with all they need to survive while enjoying their life on earth. Some creatures in turn being a food source for other creatures, including man. The circle of life some call it.

Chapter 16

I spent the next few weeks faithfully each morning taking Big Boy his food and treats. He came down to eat his food everyday. Each day I'd move closer to his food, I'd set his treat further from his food dish, closer towards where I was sitting. I talked to him while he ate, getting him used to my presence and trying to gain his trust. It became more and more obvious to me that I was not going to break through his bred in instincts within a short period of time. I might never break it completely, but I was hoping to at least gain his trust enough to be able to rescue him.

I couldn't take Big Boy his food for a few days as I had hunters coming in. When I was finally able to take him his food, Big Boy was very happy to see me, barking excitedly.

All of this searching had me asking myself a lot of questions like; Where did Big Boy come from? Is someone worried, or are they missing him? Was Big Boy raised from a puppy to protect someones livestock?

Is Big Boy a wild dog who has nowhere to call a forever home? How did Big Boy end up here, high up in this huge mountain range all by himself? Has Big Boy just lost his way home, not knowing what to do or what direction to go in? Is Big Boy protecting some animal that I haven't seen or discovered yet?

How can I possibly gain Big Boys trust to rescue him, sending him back home where he belongs? What if I can't rescue him? What is going to happen to this amazing dog? Is Big Boy going to cause harm to me or to my dogs? My mind was going 100 miles per hour trying to figure out this whole situation full of so may unknowns. I'm trying to come up with a game plan, but I'm struggling with it. It would be so much easier if I knew a little more information about Big Boy. So far, it was just a blank slate with no writing on it, just a lot of questions with no answers.

Chapter 17

I've already grown attached to Big Boy. Something that I couldn't help. I love all dogs. Big Boy needed some help from a friend, someone who could take care of his physical well being. A friend to help him hopefully get to safety, the goal being to get him back home. It was going to be a long process, but I was all in. True friends never give up on each other. True friends will go through thick and thin together, so that's my plan. My plan is to go through this with my new friend, Big Boy.

It was going to be a hard task getting Big Boys food to him over the next 3 days. My guests, or clients were coming into town to go fishing for a specific species of fish which are only found in Bear Lake. These special breed of fish are known as a Bonneville cutthroat trout. People come here to Bear Lake from all over the world to have a chance at catching one of these rare trout. Bonneville cutthroat trout take on the deep blue color that matches the stunning color of Bear Lakes water. This deep blue on their bodies is magnified by the brilliant red on their cheeks. Their bodies are covered with small black spots from their heads to their tails. Bonneville cutthroat trout boast some of the worlds biggest trout, some fish exceeding 18 pounds.

I have a deep love and admiration for all of Gods creatures. Hunting and fishing allows me to have close up encounters with so many varieties of fish, birds and animals. For me, and for many other sportsmen (and women!) it's never about just taking or killing something. It's about the excitement of the fair chase, it's about harvesting some wholesome foods to nourish and strengthen the body. There's a time and a place to harvest wild things, but there's also a time to help and protect all wild things. There's also a time to help, nurture, protect and contribute what a sportsman can to enhance all wild things from the fish to the birds to everything in between on up to big game. Simply purchasing a license to fish or hunt contributes a very large portion of the monies needed in the care and maintenance of so many different game fish and animals.

My clients would be here for 3 days, being fully accommodated from a tent camp, meals, snacks and drinks, transportation, and me being their full time fishing guide throughout their fishing adventure. I'd have to make some sacrifices in order to make sure to have time either early morning or late night to drive to where Big Boy was getting used to coming for his food. Big Boys food spot is about 2 hours from where we would be camping. Being able to continue to provide food and snacks for Big Boy was very concerning to me. It wasn't just about my providing his food, I was also concerned about Big Boy loosing any trust in me, even if that trust was a small amount that we had developed at this point.

That old saying when you run a business, 'the customer is always right' whether they are right or not, often times goes against what is really necessary. Necessary or not, my clients wanted to be on Bear Lake at first light in the mornings. So I resigned myself to the fact that I'd just have to go feed Big Boy after serving my clients their dinner, cleaning up and getting everything ready for their fishing trip early the next morning.

I didn't like having to change Big Boys feeding schedule from morning to night, but I didn't really have a choice. So for the next 3 nights I drove up and hiked in, leaving food for Big Boy. Never hearing or seeing him. Each night that I returned his food was gone that I'd placed there the night before. But there wasn't any proof that it was Big Boy eating the food. It could be any animal or bird including Magpies, crows or ravens that can find a needle in a haystack if they think it might be a free meal. My thoughts became heavy again with more questions; Was it Big Boy that ate the food? Who or what ate this food? Did some birds make off with Big Boy's food? Is Big Boy still here? Or, did he move to another place? Did his owner find Big Boy? Taking him home? I really didn't know at this point. Personally, my hopes were that his owner had come for him, taking him home to safety.

My clients last day is tomorrow, one more night of hiking in Big Boys food, then I can return to my morning schedule when it's light to bring his food. Hopefully seeing Big Boy or at least trying to find out some answers to my questions. It's going to be a long day and night with my mind making me worry about my friend Big Boy.

Chapter 18

My clients left in late afternoon, but I still had to tear down their camp, pack everything from the camp up, clean and pack up my boat and take everything back to where it was all stored. I was exhausted, but I made my last trip up the mountain to take food for my friend before I was back home and in bed.

Morning time just couldn't come fast enough. I was up way before mister sunshine had decided to share his warmth with this part of the world. My thoughts were running wild again just anticipating greeting, and hopefully seeing my new friend Big Boy if he was indeed still there.

I was in my truck and heading up the mountain before it was light. I figured that after my drive up to where Big Boy was 3 days ago, it would be light enough to hike up to my friends food dish. I'm thinking that Heavenly Father had to have been watching out for me the last few nights as I had hiked in the dark up a very steep mountainside full of everything from small 20 foot cliffs to straight up solid walls of rock leading to the base of 100 plus foot cliffs where his food dish sat. It's some very rugged country, not fit for most people to even think of trying to navigate in the dark.

I parked my truck in the now all too familiar parking spot where I had been parking for over a month now to hike in food. Again hiking up this rugged terrain. I arrived there to his dish and filled up his food. I had brought some leftover lunch meats that my clients hadn't eaten while on their fishing trip. I sat down for about an hour, periodically hollering for Big Boy with no response. I decided to head back down, I placed the left over lunch meat on the top of the kibble, then just as I had turned to begin my trek back down, I heard one loud 'woof' come from not too far away.

Here Big Boy, here Big boy, come on boy, here Big Boy come get your food. Here Big Boy I hollered out his name until here he came full boar. His stride was long, not concerned with the small cliffs, rocks, trees or bushes. Big Boy was so powerful. I stood there amazed that even with his long blonde fur his muscles could be seen flexing while his body rippled with power. After not seeing him for a few days, I realized that Big Boy was a mammoth of a dog, second to no dog I've ever seen. His fur was long, mostly pure white with spots that had been tattered or torn from his journeys in such a rugged wild place that was full of danger around every corner. Big Boy had me a little spooked as he approached, his voice a deep 'wooooooof wooooooooof wooooooof. I couldn't tell if his voice was conveying menace or excitement. Big Boy was in full stride, heading directly my way. I backed away as Big Boy made his entrance into the small clearing. He stopped, standing sideways to me with his head turned sideways not looking towards his food, but looking straight at my eyes. Big Boys eyes were stunning big brown eyes, the color of dark rich chocolate. They were full of so many expressions from love, gentleness, fear, excitement, and awareness of every single thing going on around him.

I could see no menace in his eyes or his posture, my body relaxed, my apprehension gone as I looked into his eyes. His eyes were full of truth that seemed to be looking right through me, as if he was able to see that I was no threat to him. We both stood still for what seemed like a long time before I broke eye contact and said 'Hi Big Boy, I brought you some good food, come over and get it, come on Big Boy, everything is okay, come on boy I won't hurt you. I'm here for you Big Boy.' Big Boy wouldn't make a move for his food. Backing up another short distance from him, he tentatively and very cautiously walked towards his food dish, sniffing the air while eyeballing any movement from me or anything else he was uncomfortable with.

Big Boy went for his leftover lunch meat first, scarfing it down in just a few bites. As he started in on his dog food, he started to relax. I sat down, just observing him. He finished every single bit of the food, then he slowly walked away from the empty dish, still keeping one eye on any movement from me. 'Good boy, was it good Big Boy? Are you full? Did you get enough food? Good boy, good boy.'

For me, a long 3 days of worry and concern were finally over. I relaxed knowing that Big Boy was still here, he had been eating the food that I had been leaving, and again he had a full belly. I felt that he had missed seeing me as much as I had missed seeing him. Our encounter today with the eye contact gave me hope that he was gaining some trust in me, and that it seemed he looked forward to seeing me. Giving me some hope that all of my trips here were leading to my ultimate goal of rescuing him before a harsh, unforgiving winter would set in right on top of him.

As I sat there talking to him he looked up the mountain and slowly walked away. Big Boy disappeared back up the steep mountain to somewhere that I could not see. As I stood and looked in the direction that he had gone, I wondered, could there be a trail where I could follow him up that mountain? The more I looked, the more I concluded nope, there is no way possible for a human to get up there.

Great Pyrenees are known to be exceptional mountaineers. Their reputation is legendary. From their beginning, Great Pyrenees have been known to be able to withstand harsh conditions in harsh terrain. It was now becoming obvious to me why these big dogs were known as monarchs of any conditions sent their way. After watching Big Boy come down that mountain just minutes ago, I could clearly see that if he needed to fend off any danger, it would be done with a powerful rage that would no doubt conquer any enemy, making for just another day of battle for these magnificent mountain dogs.

Chapter 19

Big Boy seemed to be doing pretty good so far. He looked healthy. I was starting to think that Big Boy wasn't stranded. My thoughts were leaning towards thinking that Big Boy was protecting something. I didn't know exactly what kind of animals were up there where he would disappear too after he ate his food everyday. But I've come to realize that Big Boy was here because he choose to be here.

Chapter 20

Big Boy wasn't a young dog, he was up there in age. I would guess him to be about 8-9. His face was full of his past experiences. To me, his face was a face of wisdom. Big Boy wasn't a follower, he is a leader of many. Big Boy is one that passes from generation to generation his knowledge down. His knowledge didn't come from a book, it came from living it first hand. Big Boy in my opinion is a rare type of soul.

Big Boy is a type who does things right. He cares about his kind, also every other kind. Big Boy believes in doing what to him is the right thing. Big Boy has incredible integrity, not in it for a pat on his back or any praise or even a thank you for that matter. He does what he does because that's his make up, this is who Big Boy strives to be. If Big Boy could speak to me, what I hear him saying is 'This is who I am, take it or leave it. I, Big Boy don't care what you think of me.'

One thing in life we all hear, or have heard about are legends. It seems most of the time the stories are all old. Legends that have lived on through time even though who or what had become legendary is long gone, past away, leaving their unmatched greatness behind like fall leaves turning into a fine dust that dissolves into the soil. But somehow their stories never become lost in the passage of time, their greatness living on long after their time on earth.

Maybe even more rare than an old legend is a living legend. If I could speak to Big Boys peers, I'm pretty sure he would be spoken of as a leader or legend. Big Boy has strayed from his group of peers to go on his journey all alone, perhaps protecting some friends, he seems to not have regards for himself. It's more about things he cares about. Big Boy without a doubt would lay down his life to do something that is so on point to him. There's no doing wrong things. To him it's always do right things. Big Boy is a living legend.

Chapter 21

Time never slows down. Time just keeps ticking away as time has passed over another week, things have stayed pretty much the same for me and for Big Boy. It's become a daily routine for us to meet every day for his mealtime. He only lets his guard down a small amount. He still greets me with sheer excitement in his voice. Big Boy has so many voices, I can hear his excitement by the sound of his greeting barks as he approaches, coming down through some treacherous terrain. He's been silent after his meals, sitting still and quiet like leaves on a tall tree when the air around it has no breeze. After awhile when he turns, heading back to where he is going, there is no prance in his steps, he puts his nose to the ground and walks off. I sense his determination, his call to duty that comes from instincts that have been ingrained into every muscle and tendon that come together to form every fiber of his being. Instincts that rule over his desire to end whatever his duty is that's holding him here on this mountain, keeping him from going home.

Chapter 22

By this time, my own 2 dogs, Spruce and Oak were wondering what this other dog is all about. Normally we would all be out on the marsh early in the mornings, hunting ducks and geese. Fulfilling my dogs instincts of hunting and retrieving. Instead we go out in the late afternoon into the evening. My faithful companions adjusting to our new hunting schedule that is so different this year.

I had started leaving them home instead of leaving them to wait in the truck while I hike up the mountain to take food to, and to have my visit with Big Boy. My thoughts were, if I can gain Big Boys trust, getting him to follow me off the mountain, and to load up in my truck, there wouldn't be any confrontation between the 3 dogs. Big Boy being a stranger, my dogs might start something they can't finish. Bottom line, I just didn't want any any of them to get hurt. It's just better to leave mine home, even though I wish they were here with me. I always feel safer when we're all together. Besides hunting season is here, they get to go on great adventures almost every day.

The weather and the season is changing, temperatures are dropping a little bit more every day. There are different smells being carried in the air, it's a sweet smell that's cool and sweet with a crispness to it. There's still so many wild berries around, it smells like a mixture of all of them put together. Late fall, early winter is such a beautiful time in northern Utah. The children are all back in school, our tourist season is over until next year. The small town is quiet, everything has slowed down as if the area has taken a step back in time, looking more like a Rockwell picture of time past. The residents slipping into a routine of simple living. There's no drama, no hustle and bustle that comes from so many people all gathered in such a small rural town. For those who live here, their world has changed so very much here in Garden City Utah.

The area where I grew up has changed, not just the physical appearance, but its morality. As each year passes, it seems to have more and more self centered people full of greed, people that have allowed themselves to be manipulated by money, lies, crooks and deceitful people. I think that the lack of morality is going on throughout all of the world. I try to believe that there will always be more good people than not so good people. I try to be an example of what it means to our Heavenly Father to live a moral life. Satan is growing stronger, pulling so many in the wrong direction. My comfort is in knowing that our Heavenly Father will prevail. He'll make sure good in the end will beat out evil. The struggles in my life make me envious of Big Boys life style. He lives so free, Big Boy lives within his heart, his heart is fed by truly precious things that fill not only his big heart, but adds up to make his entire being simply fly high, oblivious of the craziness of the people in this world. Truly pure innocence, doing only good things.

How I long to live so free! A longing that no amount of money could buy. Big Boy is for me an example of how I dream of living my life. Sure, there's set backs, hard times, ups and downs, maybe even all arounds. Struggles that are good character builders, those things that we all have, the negative things we have to work hard to overcome. Disciplining our self, we step up to the plate and then run, our stride reflecting our innermost desire to get to that new plate, safe at last from that negativity that was holding us back. Knowing that each and every obstacle that we overcome strengthens us, allowing our soul to fly a bit higher, a bit lighter, allowing us to be free from those things that are now in the past. All it took was a moment in time to change the outcome of the future, in the end changing even our eternal destination.

From spending time getting to know this amazing dog Big Boy, within such a short amount of time, I have learned so many things of importance to implement into my own life. Sometimes, if we all just pay a little more attention to little things, they become huge things that Heavenly Father has subtly placed in our lives to bring us closer to knowing Him. Bringing us closer to living our lives for Him, which brings peace into our life knowing that if we allow Him, he directs our lives.

Chapter 23

Winter is almost here. Before long, there will be a pure white blanket of snow covering up all of northern Utah. When winter comes, it comes quickly, when winter gets here it doesn't leave for about 5 months. Northern Utah will have some minus degree temperatures that are as severe as any state in this country. There's a place about 6 miles from where Big Boy is located, it's called Peter sinks. It's 8,100 feet above sea level. Due to temperature inversions that will trap freezing cold air, it by far holds records of some of Utah's coldest temperatures. In 1985 at Peter sinks, temperatures plummeted to minus 69. It was the second coldest temperature ever recorded in all lower 48 states. This is very concerning to me right now. Mostly because Big Boy is basically right next door to Peter sinks.

I realize that Great Pyrenees are built for harsh conditions to a certain point. But 70 below zero is beyond cold, especially with no shelter to help hold the heat in his body. Big Boy is a big dog, he eats a pretty big meal that I bring him everyday. When winter comes full force, there will be no way to get food to him. This rescue mission needs to right now take some big steps moving forward, or Big Boys chance of surviving to fight another day are abruptly going to come to an end.

Sometimes, I wish even though dogs don't speak our language, that there was a better way for us to understand and to communicate with each other. Kind of like a silent language which we could all understand. It's hard for me, knowing that soon Big Boy was going to be in big trouble. If we could just communicate, it would be a tremendous help in this whole ordeal. Big Boy had been around a block or two in his life, but this block was leading not around, it was leading to a dead end alley with sheer walls where there were no exits leading out. If somehow this could just be expressed to Big Boy, maybe between us we could come to a conclusion to make a plan for escape.

Chapter 24

Things were getting pretty complicated for my simple mind. One thing I know for sure about true friends, is that there is no such thing as the phrase 'I'm going to give up.' Being a true friend meant there was no giving up, ever. True friends stick together until the crisis comes to an end. Sometimes it never ends long after the crisis is over. Our friendship needing the care and support that we provide to each other.

My phone just buzzed with a weather forecast, letting me know there's going to be 4 consecutive days of snow above 6,000 feet with rain or rain/snow mix in the valleys. It would be here late tonight, continuing on throughout this weekend. Logan canyon is a pretty narrow, winding mountain pass with a road to match. Once it starts snowing, the ground will be cooled, the falling snow will stick and build up. Some winters there will be over 20 feet of snow, completely covering even tall trees. The snow turning the 8,000 foot tall mountain tops into a smooth landscape of pure white.

In Utah they brag about having some of the greatest snow on earth. There's dozens of world class ski resorts in Utah. As the crow flies, Big Boy is located about 10 miles from one. Prior to a ski resort being built, one thing that's looked for is an area with a large amount of average snowfall, creating enormous depths of snow. Ski resort owners are in the business to make money. They want to have early snow depths that enable them to open their ski resorts as early as possible to start generating profits.

Not only is Big Boy within a few miles of an area with recorded sub zero temperatures, he's also in a place where the snow is going to come early, and it's going to get deep fast. Big Boy has a lot of strikes against him. It's going to take a home run to get him out of here.

Chapter 25

Another day is almost here, morning would be here soon. It's raining as the weather predicted, it's going to be a cold wet day. I have hunters coming into town that I will be taking out on a hunt for Canadian Geese, so I'm up and preparing everything for them to have as successful of a hunt as I can provide. I can't take Big Boys food at the time that I normally do, today it would be late afternoon.

Laying in a soaking wet blind out here in a field gives a person a whole new perspective than spending a cold day inside watching TV does. It gives me the opportunity to witness first hand how the colder temperatures and the snow force a change in all of the wild creatures habits. It forces them to change how they forage in search of food. As I lay here, geese are hopefully headed to this grain field in search of food. In cold weather, food becomes extremely vital to their survival. For the wild creatures food becomes warmth. They don't have our luxuries of opening up a cupboard or refrigerator to grab a yummy snack. They don't have a knob or a button to push to turn up a thermostat that signals a furnace to provide heat, they have no fireplace or wood stove to simply throw a log into to warm them up. There's no insulated walls around them, or a roof over their heads to provide shelter. Heavenly Father has provided His wild creatures with warm coats, and with forage foods that allows them to seek out a survival in this harsh environment. Wild creatures do live free, but it all comes at a high cost of calories when wintertime is here. Big Boy is opening my eyes to the reality of the meaning of survival of the fittest, Big Boy is very fit. But can he survive wintertime in northern Utah with the cards stacked against him?

The hunt was very successful, my clients filling their limits for the day earlier than I had expected. I've parked my trailer that's full of goose decoys, unloaded the hunting gear and loaded up my back pack that is filled with kibble for Big Boy. I packed a good sized bowl of some left over duck, goose, rice and sweet peas that I am taking today for Big Boy's treats along with a fist full of large size dog biscuits.

The rain turned to light snow soon after heading up the canyon road. Not enough snow has accumulated on the roads surface yet to require snow plow drivers to be out keeping the road passable. The snow reminds me that I need to remember to put a snow shovel or at the least a square shovel into the back of my truck. Once the snow starts getting deep, I'm going to need to clear out my parking spot along the road below where Big Boy is located.

Arriving at my parking spot, there is is about an inch of snow now on the roadway, and about 2 inches of snow on the side of the road where there is gravel, but at least 8 inches has accumulated on the mountainside. My ascent is slower than normal, but the hike wasn't too difficult.

Big Boy is laying next to his food dish when I arrive, still, alert and watching me intently as I approached. If I wouldn't have known to watch for him, my eyes could have overlooked his still form that blended into the snow. I stopped, catching my breath from making the hike, while admiring my friend. Big Boy looked royal laying there, like a sentinel proudly guarding a king's throne. 'Hey Big Boy! Have you been waiting for me? Sorry that I'm late, but to make it up to you I've brought you a yummy bowl of leftovers!' Big Boy stood up, and shook the layer of snow off of his long coat. No wonder he had blended in so well!

I took the leftovers out of my pack, removed the lid and sat the bowl down on the snow covered ground. Big Boy moved over to the side, circling back behind me as I approached his food dish. The dish was full of snow so I scooped it out and filled it with his kibble. By now he had finished his bowl of leftovers, so as I moved away from his food dish, he approached.

I sat and watched him eat, talking to him as he ate as I normally did. The snow is starting to fall pretty heavily, so I take my leave and head back to my truck. When I arrive back to my truck I see that there is now about 2 inches of snow on the roadway. A snowplow truck passes me by heading the direction of my home as I clean the snow off of my windshield. Out loud I voice my thanks to the driver for being out in this storm to provide a safer road for me to travel home.

It's raining lightly in the valley as I pull into my driveway. I can hear my dogs jumping and barking excitedly as they hear my key in the door. It's good to be safely home.

Chapter 26

The next morning while sitting and drinking a cup of coffee, I'm thinking about ideas to try to gain Big Boys trust. It's going to be hard breaking what he was bred and raised to do. He's an older dog that's followed his instincts his whole life.

As I was pondering on new ideas, it had started a pretty heavy rain outside. There was no view of Bear Lake, everything was getting socked in by some really thick clouds emptying their load of moisture. The outside temperatures were still in the mid 30's, not even freezing yet, but at 8,000 feet high up in altitude, I'm pretty sure that it's been snowing all night.

As I've said, Logan canyon is not a good road to drive when it's snowing. It's very slick with a lot of blind corners. It also can get very windy that causes snow drifts across the roadway. There is a pretty good sized freestone river that runs side by side the road for about halfway through this canyon. Steep cliffs drop hundreds of feet on either side where the sheer rock stops right into the Logan river. There are a lot of accidents with some of them being terminal for some drivers and passengers. I try to avoid it when it has been snowing a lot, or if the road is iced up. It's going to be a challenge driving to my parking spot today.

I head out, and sure enough, about halfway there, the rain had turned to snow. It wasn't a really heavy snow, it had big snowflakes but not really full of heavy water, more of a dry, fluffy snow. The plow trucks had done a great job of removing the snow from the roadway, and they had spread ice melt and sand, especially thick on hills and curves. I arrived and set out with my filled pack.

As I got close to where Big Boys food dish sat, I noticed that there was about 6 inches of snow covering up Big Boys steep trail down to his food. He greeted me with a different type of bark, slowing his approach as he came down off the mountain. It appeared that he was being cautious with his footing, trying to pick and choose a safe way down. Big Boy is so smart, I was thinking if he gets hurt, it won't be a very good thing. I'll bet if I could read his mind, this same thought was going through Big Boys mind.

I had filled his dish, without any hesitation, Big Boy went straight to his food. Normally he is more cautious, watching for any movements I make. This time he wasn't cautious at all, to me it was a good thing. Maybe Big Boy was gaining some trust in me. Maybe he is coming to know that there was no threat from me, that I'm here as his friend, my desire to do nothing but help him.

Big Boy finished his meal, for once slowing down, taking his time to eat instead of just gulping it down. He also did not have his focus on immediately turning around heading back up to where he was going after eating. Big Boy scratched at the snow covered ground, he sat down, looking my way with his eyes conveying a gentle, thankful look. Eyes that seemed to be free of any mistrust. He seemed to be looking at my soul through my eyes, realizing that my heart was true. Big Boy looked so tired, I wished that he would just curl up, and fall into a deep sleep while I watched over him, trusting me to make sure that he was safe while sleeping. This pure soul deserved a worry free rest, a rest free from being worried about anyone else sleeping safely.

Big Boy sat for a long time, seemingly struggling with a decision of allowing himself to forget that he had his duty to do. Seeming to make his decision, Big Boy stood up, taking his eyes away from mine and turning his head back upwards. Seeming like he was looking for a safe way to climb back up this unforgiving steep mountain. Then he was on his way, I watched him as he purposely picked his path upwards until he had disappeared once again. Leaving me to wonder again just what it was that had such a strong hold on Big Boy. What was it that has him determined to stay here on this mountain?

Chapter 27

There was more snow in the forecast, at least for 2 more days, maybe even 3. It was a slick slow moving road for me on my way home. How I was wishing Big Boy was riding in the truck with me, sitting right next to me. Both of us on our way home.

My dogs were happy when my truck pulled in. They were both wagging their tails, barking while waiting to greet me as I walked in. After greeting them, once again my thoughts were full of just how much I love them both. Bringing me to being so upset with anyone who could own such a loving animal like a dog, yet let them suffer trying to survive on their own like Big Boy was doing.

Us people are so fortunate, we have other people, family and friends to count on. Dogs aren't always so fortunate, dogs that do have good owners have us to count on. Thinking of me and my dogs made it more clear to me, that all that Great Pyrenees had was me, and there was no way I was going to let Big Boy down. In my opinion his owner had let him down whether intentionally or unintentionally didn't matter. Absolutely no way, no how would I ever do such a thing as abandon my own dogs, or in this instance, even a dog that may belong to someone else. Big Boy was stuck with me, his new friend for life.

Chapter 28

Overnight mother nature had dropped an additional 6 inches of snow up here on the mountain. I'm afraid that this high up in this mountain range winter was settling in for good.

As I got to where I'd been meeting Big Boy everyday, again he was already here waiting for me. He had been curled up sleeping, standing up greeting me with no barks, just a very tired face. 'Big Boy, what's going on? Are you doing okay? Are you hungry? Come on Big Boy, lets go home.' I turned to walk away, patting my leg. 'Let's go Big Boy, come on Bog Boy.' Big Boy only followed for a few steps, then stopped letting out a long drawn out 'woooooof.' He was ready to eat, but not ready to go home with me. After Big Boy ate, he didn't stick around. But this time as he left, he didn't take his normal pathway back up the mountain. He instead walked pretty close to me, and headed in another direction. I followed him with my eyes for maybe 100 yards, then he turned and headed up into an area with even more steep jagged cliffs. Soon he was gone from my sight, disappearing as he blended in with the white snow.

After pondering about why his course up the mountain had changed, my thoughts again were wondering, trying to figure out why or what was driving him. Causing him to refuse to leave, always heading back up that mountain everyday. Why did Big Boy take a different trail up there today? My mind was stumped again.

I needed to figure this out, I needed to know the reason why Big Boy was so set in remaining here. I needed an answer. I decided to go back to my truck and get my binoculars, then climb up an adjacent mountain to try to see where his trail was leading up to. At this point any information would be so helpful in trying to figure out this situation with this dog that I call Big Boy.

Chapter 29

Grabbing my binoculars out of my truck, I headed up an adjacent mountain, on my way up to locate a good view point nearby where I could try to follow Big Boys new trail up what has become his mountain.

After hiking for about an hour, I found what I hoped was a good viewpoint. I could see his trail, as I followed his trail I could see that it zigzagged, going up into a group of small trees or berry bushes. The trail seemed to continue on, turned, and met up with what appeared to be a main trail that headed up the steep terrain towards the top, and then over Big Boys mountain. Big Boys zigzagging trail stopped at the clump of trees or bushes. There has to be a reason for his trail to just stop there at these small trees or berry bushes. Maybe there was something I couldn't see, or something that the snow was camouflaging that left no way for him to go through or around them?

As I watched the mountainside, I saw movement, here came Big Boy heading towards one of many small bushes. I'm pretty sure these bushes were wild rose bushes, I could see what looked like rose hips on the branches. Rose hips will last all winter long, never getting overripe like so many other wild berries or fruits do. Rose hips are good to eat all winter long, staying eatable into early next spring. Big Boy approached this rose bush, about midway down the bush, there was a branch that was full of rose hips. He broke off this branch, setting it aside until he had broken off about a dozen branches, Big Boy had made a pretty good pile of small branches that were loaded with rose hips. He then scooped them all up with his mouth, then turning around he headed back across his trail and disappeared again into the trees. As I watched from the adjacent mountain, Big Boy returned to the rose bush 3 more times, breaking off about a dozen small branches of rose hips each time. Just enough to fill his mouth, he seemed to be trying to not carry too much at a time back up his mountain. What's he doing? Is he making himself a shelter? Or perhaps a bed to sleep on? Am I not feeding him enough food? Is Big Boy still hungry, now turning to eating wild rose hips?

What's he up to? I'll start feeding him more food, waiting until he's finished eating then fill his dish up again. There's no way that I'm going to let Big Boy be in need of food or ever go hungry.

As my thinking had gone, all I could come up with was that Big Boy was hungry. Well, 'click' a light bulb just lit up pretty bright like 'ummmmmm' Big Boy isn't hungry at all, but his friends are very hungry! He's got to have something he's going back up that mountain every day for. Yep, he's protecting some kind of animals up there. Big Boy just cleared up so many of my questions when he kept carrying one mouthful of rose hips at a time back into those trees. He had been taking care of his friends this whole time. Somehow, some of the sheep that Big Boy was responsible for had gotten stranded and were unable to go up or down this mountain. Maybe a summer rainstorm had caused a boulder to fall, maybe a large tree had fallen, what ever had happened, something had blocked off the way that they had come in, preventing them from returning the way that they had come in, obviously blocking the only way out, trapping them on this mountain.

No wonder I couldn't get him to leave with me. He wasn't going anywhere by himself. It was that rule of loving others more than we love ourselves, a love that was so alive inside of Big Boys heart. A hero's heart that beats only inside the hearts of those with a soul of willing sacrifice, a heart that protects and serves, protecting lives and giving others their life or their freedom at their expense. Making heroic sacrifices every second of every day. The finest men, women and dogs in our world, including our police and first responders, those in our armed forces, all of those who refuse to leave a man behind even if it means jeopardizing or loosing their lives. I think Big Boy is exactly like they are, he was in it to win it, it was all or nothing to Big Boy. Big Boy was leaving with his friends all together, or Big Boy wasn't leaving at all.

Now I have another problem, just how am I going to get food to Big Boy's friends? For some reason his friends aren't able to come down to eat with Big Boy, or even get off this mountain. There is no way for me to know why or how or even how many sheep are stranded. I'm worried, what am I going to do?

Chapter 30

As I drive home I'm thinking about how winter days grow shorter, everyday becomes dark a little bit earlier. In Utah there's a time change in fall, we set our clocks backwards 1 hour. Then in springtime our clocks go forward 1 hour. They say it makes summer days longer with more sunlight. Winter days are just as long but with less sunlight. It seems kind of senseless to me. I don't think that Mr. Sun sets his clock back an hour...hehehe. Sunshine is so good for us all, humans and animals, that vitamin D we get from sunshine is healthy, it helps with our immune system and keeps us from being depressed. I know that freezing cold temperatures with longer dark days don't fill me with joy. Sometimes it makes me wonder who makes these decisions; Like what are you people thinking when you do things like this?

On my way home I'm thinking about how or where I'm going to get food for Big Boys friends. I know where there were a lot of not only rose hips, but wild apples trees with perfectly ripe small branches of Johnathan apples on them. This time of the year wild apples are as sweet as they get. They are full of juice, they explode in your mouth with every bite of pure goodness. Many times I've picked a 10 gallon bucket of them for myself. And of course some extras for a yummy treat when I see horses along back roads in my travels. It's always fun to stop and give beautiful horses a handful of sweet apples. It's probably like a piece of candy to them. Some horses know I stop when I have good treats, so when my blue truck turns, and is coming down a dirt road heading their way they get all excited, twisting circles and bucking while trotting my way.

That's it! I'm going to stop at the trees and break off some branches with 4 or 5 small apples on them, then I'll tie them together in a small bunch that Big Boy can carry back up to his friends. Hopefully helping put a little something in their empty bellies to keep them a bit warmer during these chilly days. Days that are leading into even more chilly nights that are coming sooner with this time change. Bringing darkness in my opinion way too early.

I stopped and broke off about 20 small branches, using fishing line to make some bundles. I decided there's still enough time left in this day, so why not take these small branches of delicious apples back up, leaving them next to Big Boy's food dish. It would be interesting to see if Big Boy could figure it out, gathering them up and delivering them to his friends for a mid day snack. Back up the mountain and back up the trail I hike with my load of branches. There was no sign of Big Boy, he probably had called it off for the day.

Calling it a day sounded like a great idea to me, a warm house with a hot meal was on my mind. Have a good night Big Boy, sleep tight my friend, I'll see you tomorrow.

After dinner, it was bedtime for us. My dogs are pretty spoiled, they have their own bedroom with a big bed and a couch with puffy comforters on it. For some reason, both of them seem to think that my bed just must be more comfortable. They insist on getting some scratches and loves. Sometimes a talk or bedtime story about my day. Then off to sleep they drift atop my bed, making me sleep all curled up in uncomfortable positions, or just barely hanging on to a small corner of my mattress, sometimes causing me to fall off 'my' bed that they have totally taken over. Both dogs were dreaming, making all kinds of grunts, snorts, growls, even some barks or howls. As I laid there, my friend Big Boy was on my mind. What kind of primitive bed was he sleeping in? Or maybe he had no bed and was just curled up in a ball trying to stay warm. Was Big Boy able to snuggle with his friends?

Was he so smart that he had gathered pine boughs, leaves or grass to insulate his body while he sleeps? One thought comes to mind, most predators hunt more actively at night time, it gives them some cover in helping them surprise their prey, giving them a big advantage on being successful in their survival. This brought me to wonder; Does Big Boy sleep through night time at all? He's got to be sleeping sometime. Was it during mid day? My dogs have it so easy compared to what my friend

Big Boy is dealing with every single day. Thinking about him gives a new found respect to all wild living things, especially in wintertime.

Unable to sleep, I glance out my window. It's snowing now, there's no sounds. My belly is full, my house is warm, my bed is comfortable. But my mind is none of them, it's racing around a million miles an hour. If my mind was a race car competing in the Daytona 500, it would not only win this race, it would lap all other race cars time and time again.

Sometimes I wonder, why do I even care? Why not just turn my shoulder, going on with my day to day life not stressing or worrying about just another dog? My answer is simple, there's no such thing as just another dog. Dogs to me are God's foremost creature sent here to love while protecting us all during our lives, spending their whole lives doing so. Dogs must be God's foremost creatures. He gave them his name, only he spelled it backwards.

Chapter 31

Morning came soon, not much sleep for me as I was way too heavy in thought. It had dropped maybe 3 inches of fresh snow down low, Bear Lake Valley was turning into a winter wonderland. I load up my pack, before I load up into my truck I grab a shovel as I head out to go see my friend.

As I'm again driving to the apple trees to break off more branches, my views of the snow covered landscape remind me that when winter is gone, this valley will flood with people coming to recreate on the lake and in the mountains where they can escape the heat. But during this season, snow brings joy and new adventures with so many fun activities that are welcomed by winter enthusiasts from all over this world. They come to ski, snowmobile, ice fish or just explore Utah's perfect snow. Unfortunately, snow also brings hardships, starvation and freezing cold temperatures to all wild creatures living in it. Hopefully most of them survive to see another bountiful spring, summer and fall where they will all thrive preparing their bodies for the next years oncoming winter.

As I drive up this mountain pass, I see trucks and snowmobile trailers, there's a hill where children are sledding and I see a few cross country skiers. There's getting to be quite a bit of snow up here in the mountains.

When I get to my parking spot, I was glad to have a shovel. When the snow plows push the snow from roadways, it creates a big berm blocking off any pull offs, including my parking spot where I can safely park my truck and leave it for a few hours while I'm feeding and watching Big Boy. I was excited to see if Big Boy had figured out that those branches of apples were for him to carry back up to help his friends with some good food.

I make my hike up, and again, Big Boy was waiting. He must have been there for quite awhile, as when standing up there was about an inch of snow across his back on his pure white coat. He acted like it wasn't a big deal, shaking it off in just one shake. He greeted me with a soft 'rooo rooo roooo' that isn't a bark, but more like he was talking to me saying 'thank you.'

I set the bundle of apple branches down, Big Boy side stepped a few feet as I approached, letting me come on by to fill up his food dish. It seemed everyday he was growing more trust in me. I cleaned the snow out of the inside of his food dish, as well as a ways around it. As I cleared away the snow I uncovered some apples. I was disappointed for a second until I realized that there were only a few apples, not the full branches. Wait a minute, there were only a few apples still there, this is great news! His friends had gotten some good food in their bellies. Big Boy was such a smart dog! He just amazes me. He had figured out that I had left the apple branches for his friends!

As I stood there, still amazed at this dog, Big Boy ate about half of his food, then grabbing one of the bundles of the small branches full of apples, he headed across to his trail, a proud yet determined look in his eyes as he headed upwards towards where his friends were waiting for him to bring them their meal.

A short distance up his trail, Big Boy stopped, still within my sight he shook and 2 apples fell from the branches. Then he walked another 40 or 50 feet and dropped the branch with the remaining apples. I stood there with a puzzled look on my face, thinking why would Big Boy do this? Didn't he want to carry some fresh apples to his friends? Why is he dropping apples everywhere? Well it was worth a try, maybe he had gotten enough rose hips that his friends were full, not needing anymore food?

Big Boy came back and grabbed another bundle. Off he went up his trail as I watched puzzled, wondering what he was doing. As I watched, he stopped just up from where he dropped the last bundle. Again he shook some apples off before he continued going up the trail further. Here came that light bulb turning on in my small brain again, no way, no way! There is no way a dog is this smart! In a mind that was able to reason, this made perfectly good sense. Big Boy was leaving apples scattered on his trail to lead his friends down off this mountain to safety. Would it work? Well Big Boy in my mind just went from being a smart dog to being a brilliant dog.

I decided to leave Big Boy to complete his rescue idea. I was afraid that if I was there that I would spook his friends and prevent them from following the trail of apples down the mountain.

I hiked back down to my truck, my hopes high that Big Boys plan would work and that tomorrow we'd all be going home!

I didn't stop to get more branches of apples on my way home. I'm hoping that Big Boy is successful with his plan, then tomorrow we'd be focusing on getting them off the mountain and to a safe place where they would have plenty of food.

I got home and loaded up my dogs and my shotgun, hooked the boat to my truck and headed out to do some duck hunting. I had to keep my mind off how Big Boy was doing with luring his friends down the mountain.

We had a successful hunt, fresh duck cooked and covered in wild current jelly was on the menu! The dogs helped me eat the ducks while we lounged on the couch watching some favorite TV shows.

It was soon bedtime and I couldn't wait until tomorrow!

Chapter 32

I couldn't sleep at all that night. I was up pacing and looking at the clock every 15 minutes as if somehow my pacing could will the time to pass faster. At 3:30 I couldn't wait any longer. It was only 3 hours to sunrise. I decided to head up the mountain and wait in my truck until it was light enough for me to see to hike up.

My dogs both watched me from their bed as I packed up to head out. They must be wondering what's going on, and they must be tired from watching me pace all night.

I drove up to the all too familiar parking spot. There had been no new snow so I was able to park without shoveling snow. I sat in my truck with the heater going, listening to music. I must have dozed off, when I woke up it was light enough to see! I shouldered my pack and off I went anxious to see if Big Boys plan had worked, and if they were all waiting for me by the food dish.

My anticipation pushed my legs faster than normal, I felt like I made the hike in just a short few minutes. As the area where the food dish came into my sight my heart sank. There were no sheep, and no Big Boy to greet me. Full of disappointment I sat down in the snow.

What's wrong with his friends? Why wouldn't they follow a trail full of sweet apples leading them to safety where I could rescue them? Taking them back home with me where they would all be safe? It wouldn't be long until they are all stranded, including my friend Big Boy. Time is about over, soon time will close it's window, opening up another window for a wintertime where the snow will become too deep.

I can't give up, Big Boy is a good team member, between us we both could figure this out. I wasn't going to abandon Big Boy, while Big Boy wasn't going to abandon his friends. In a way, myself and Big Boy had been reading each others mind. Both playing from a silent game plan to win this game of getting everyone off of this mountain safely before this window shuts our plans completely down.

Our weather forecast was calling for a few days of sunshine with a 20% chance of snow. It was looking like Big Boy was was going to get a small break. There is still a possibly that if I keep bringing apples, Big Boy can keep using them, working on his idea of baiting his friends to come down from high up on his mountain. Maybe, just maybe our plan would work, all coming together just in the nick of time.

I filled Big Boy's food dish and headed down to my truck. It's still very early, I'm going to drive back down and get more branches of apples.

For the next 3 days straight, I brought more branches of apples along with kibbles to fill his dish. Big Boy continued scattering the apples all over his trail. We both had high hopes of our plan working. But after 3 days working together, we still didn't have any good results.

It had warmed back up a little bit, it was back around 50 degrees, melting a little bit of snow. It wouldn't last long, there was more coming in this week.

What is wrong with Big Boy's friends? What are they thinking by not coming down off that mountain? Is there just one friend, or more? Is he or she injured? Maybe for some reason they are not able to get down this mountain. Maybe Big Boy's friends can't get down?

If they are hurt, maybe they are stranded? Maybe they are boxed in between huge boulders? I really don't know, all I can do is think about the many possibilities while wondering what's really going on here. I'd love to help, but how can I help when it's too steep for me to climb? I'm not able to physically get to where they are at.

Chapter 33

My goose hunters had canceled for this week due to the incoming winter storm that's due to hit tonight. There's a radio channel that gives state wide weather warnings, reporting on road conditions with travel warnings due to heavy snowfall followed up by high winds. This station is advising no unnecessary travel for good reason. When it snows hard in Logan Canyon, sometimes several feet in just one single storm, the snow on the roads is removed quickly by half a dozen giant snow plows that work 7 days a week, 24 hours per day. What makes it really dangerous, causing conditions that make it impossible to go through, are the high winds that blow the snow into huge drifts that can't be plowed without some help from a front end loader to bust through, and scoop the snow aside.

Another winter hazard that comes with the high winds are what's called white out's where you loose all sight. You can't see even a foot in front of you, the snow on the ground and the falling snow are blown to where everything around you becomes completely white, disorienting you to where you loose all sense of direction. You can't see where the road is located. You are forced to stop, before ending up being involved in an accident or stuck in a snow bank. The possibility of going off the road and over a cliff, or ending up mid river with freezing cold water filling up your car in just a few short seconds are all possible if you go off the road.

Throughout the night it became so silent. I live in an old building that was built in about 1935. It was built out of cinder blocks which over time have gotten small gaps, holes or cracks in the mortar holding them in place. It's like a wind tunnel in my house even in a light breeze you can feel cool air coming in.

When I can't hear any sounds or feel a breeze inside, normally it means we are having a heavy wet snow that is covering up my house, sticking to the block and filling in all the small gaps, holes or cracks.

It was a long cold winter night even for me.

Chapter 34

Morning is here now, and I was right, it had snowed over a foot of heavy wet snow. After shoveling out my driveway, I headed toward Logan Canyon only to see flashing lights from 2 highway patrol vehicles. There were several accidents including an 18 wheeler that had jack knifed coming down the steep snow covered canyon road.

One of the highway patrolmen approached my truck, I rolled down my window and he tells me that Logan canyon is closed until further notice. O boy, this is terrible, it's just what's not needed right now. What's Big Boy going to do for food today? It's out of my hands for today. Big Boy should be fine, hopefully, since I'd been feeding him extra kibbles and extra treats maybe he hadn't finish off all of his food from yesterday. Some days when I went to fill up his food there had still been some left that he hadn't eaten.

I figured that I'd try again this afternoon. I drove back up about noon, then at 2:00 then the last time just before 4:00. Even if it was open at 4:00, I'd have been risking driving up the mountain with the continuing snowfall and darkness approaching at about 5:30. The road was still closed down, and was now snowing even harder than last night. There was almost 2 feet of heavy wet snow sticking here in the valley already, getting deeper with every minute of time passing by.

We're so blessed here in Northern Utah. We have our snow plow crew, first responders, police force, and many more good people that work together for all of our well being. Everyone drops their personal things that need to be done, but can be put off or delayed to come together as one unstoppable force. Helping each other without thinking about just themselves.

Chapter 35

About noon the following day the road was finally open. Before heading up the mountain, I stopped and bought a box of the large dog biscuits and a package of beef round steak. I stopped by an apple tree and broke off several branches with apples attached.

Finally getting to where Big Boy is, taking 2 hours digging out my parking spot from about 3 feet of new snow, just hoping my luck might change. I was not only hoping to see Big Boy close by his food dish, but also praying his friends had followed him, all waiting together to be rescued.

Well that's not happening, there were no friends or Big Boy waiting for me. Big Boy was nowhere in sight. Here Big Boy, come on Big Boy, here Big Boy. Where are you Big Boy? Come on Boy. There were no greeting barks, just silence as more snow drops flake by flake adding to the already deep snow.

There's Big Boy! Here comes my friend! Big Boy was back on his old trail, heading straight down towards me. As I've told you, Big Boy is a big tall dog, but all I could see is his head and his tail. His tail sticking up like a white flag of surrender waving in the wind. I could see that Big Boy wasn't able to easily walk through this wet snow, all he could do is become his own snowplow, crashing through, making a pathway. The snow was deeper than Big Boy was tall. He was grunting, breathing hard while working his way slowly towards me. Big Boy would forge through for about 20 yards, then sit regaining his breath and gathering up energy to move forward again, then again, then again until he at last made it to me. Hi Big Boy! You made it! Come over here Big Boy, I've got some good food for you. Come on Big Boy, come over here.

I took one of the round steaks from the package of 3 steaks, I reached my hand full of raw meat out towards him, trying to tempt him to come closer to me than he had ever been. He refused to take it from my hand. My intention at this point in time was to try to coax him close enough to where I could get a hold of him. Maybe he sensed my thoughts of just taking a big chance by grabbing him, hopefully being able to keep him from biting me, and get him down the mountain where I could get him back to my truck where a portable dog crate was awaiting his arrival. It was getting critical that he gets off this mountain. Dogs are incredible, they sense so many things that us humans will never be able to do. Dogs sense good things and not so good things.

Dogs are kind of like a super natural being. Everything about them is better than us humans. Pound for pound, they are stronger than us, they can endure conditions that would crush us. Dogs are full of an unconditional love which is unmatched by us. They work hard for no pay. Dogs during their short lives just seem to give 110% of themselves to all of us, there's no doubt in my mind they would give their life to save ours. This was one thing I'm really concerned about with Big Boy, it had been on my mind ever since Big Boy had carried those rose hips back up to feed his friends. Big Boy wasn't going to leave without his friends even if it meant giving his life while trying to feed them and keep them safe.

My love for dogs has grown to a new level. Big Boy whether he knows it or not, is an icon. He's in a way becoming a mentor to me. Big Boy stands for what's important or what really matters in life. Big Boy stands for truth with no lies or underlying conspiracies to put himself in a better position. This is so very rare, it just doesn't happen very often in humans. I am unable to explain my admiration for Big Boy at this point.

I'm glad that Big Boy sensed that I was going to try to grab him. As I thought more about taking action first instead of thinking about what my actions would, or could have caused. By grabbing Big Boy, taking him away would still have left his friends stranded and in big trouble without him there to feed and protect them. Big Boy wouldn't have even thought of doing that to me or anyone else if the shoe was on his foot. Now it was crystal clear, my intentions needed to remain inline with Big Boys intentions. All there is to be done is the right thing. It was still about saving Big Boy, but it also included honoring his wishes, which were 'we are all leaving together, or we're not leaving at all.'

Big Boy grabbed a mouthful of apple branches, I watched as he struggled going back up his trail. He would get going forward, then his back legs would sink down making a steep wall in front of him that he would have to climb over time after time. After what seemed like an eternity, he disappeared once again, I knew that he would not give up until he was high up where his friends were awaiting his safe arrival and their much needed food.

Chapter 36

One of my friends has a big ranch, he has 2 great Pyrenees for pets. He's been so helpful helping my understanding of this breed of dogs. He also had many other animals which were fed bales of fresh alfalfa harvested from his land. They were 60 pound bales that could be carried into where Big Boy would come for his food. Even though leaving branches full of small sweet apples didn't work so well in luring his friends down that mountain, they did provide food for his friends. It's possible that the snow has gotten deep enough to cover over what ever it was that was blocking the way down.

I'm hoping that maybe green alfalfa would do a better job of luring the sheep down if it's now possible. If Big Boy did what he did, making a trail full of green alfalfa that his friends are used to being fed in the winter, it would trigger them to make a move to a different spot that maybe would make this great rescue attempt become possible.

Chapter 37

nxiety is really starting to set in. I'm really getting concerned about the snow getting too deep. Misses winter seems to have made her mind up. There wasn't anything that could be said or done at this point to even try to change Misses winter's mind. Her mind was clearly and knowingly made up. It was now her time to show off her true heaven sent beauty. Misses winter is so full of unbelievable power. She brings a fresh pure white blanket covering almost everything in her path. In a sense, Misses winter is covering up Heavenly Father's creations, giving them all a time of rest while shedding all of last years happenings.

In early springtime when Mister Sunshine has a little talk with Misses winter, they both agree to disagree but still be good friends. Misses winter wants to show off her pure white blanket that covers almost everything for what seems to be an eternity. That's what she lives for. On the other hand, Mister sunshine wants to do what he lives for. He warms the world up bringing new beautiful things back to life so they can live and show off their beauty with everyone. Mister sunshine has a lot of friends, sometimes maybe he gets in a big hurry not only to showoff, but to greet his other friends like Mister and Misses Spring, Summer and Fall.

Chapter 38

Today when I hike into Big Boys food dish, I'm going to bring in a bale of alfalfa hay. It's going to be a huge chore for me to get the 60 pound bale up the steep terrain.

I hiked in with the bale of hay. It was definitely a huge chore! I lost my footing on the snow covered steep terrain a few times, and it was slow going to get the heavy bale up to the semi level area where Big Boys food dish was located. Now all that I could do was wait for tomorrow to find out what Big Boy would do.

Driving back home I'm thinking, wondering what Big Boy would do with that bale of alfalfa hay, again anxiety kicked in. What would Big Boy do? Would he carry the alfalfa to his friends? Would he make a trail of hay for them to follow down to safety? Would he do anything at all? Is there going to be a happy ending for Big Boy? Will Big Boy perish high up on this rocky mountainside full of steep cliffs, trying his best to save his friends with me trying my best at saving him?

Chapter 39

It was pretty much a sleepless night. Again, Big Boy was heavy on my mind so I left early, anxious to see what Big Boy had done, if anything with the bale of hay.

When arriving at my pull off, I decided to first hike to that lookout point across from where Big Boy was at. I trudged through about 3 ½ to 4 feet of snow covered steep terrain, finally making it to my birds eye view of Big Boys mountain across from me. Bringing up my optics, I scanned every direction, looking not only for Big Boy but also looking for any sign of his friends.

It wasn't long when I just couldn't believe my eyes. Big Boy was hauling a big wafer of alfalfa hay up his mountain! I wonder if he has been hauling what he could fit in his mouth, small portions at a time all night long? His trail was cut deep, the snow on the trail was tramped down from his many trips down and back up the mountain. There were small pieces of visible green spots from the alfalfa hay falling from his mouth.

As I watched, Big Boy headed through a thicket of trees, just to one side of a steep cliff that looked like it would be nearly impossible to climb. There were trees covering most of that area that I could see with my binoculars. Big Boy made it to his destination. When he arrived, he dropped his load of alfalfa hay. It hadn't even had time to fall from his mouth when 3 sheep appeared, rushing in with driving hunger. Three friends! Big Boy has three friends up there. Big Boy had done it! Big Boy had brought his friends their much needed food! I was amazed, there's no way, no how this was even believable! If it wasn't witnessed by myself, what this amazing dog who is named Big Boy has done to save his friends, there's no way it would have been something I would have even considered believable.

Chapter 40

As I stood there dumbfounded, I thought about everything that this amazing, unbelievable dog had done for his friends. Big Boy had gathered branches of wild rose hips, he had taken apples, he had tried to make trails of the sweet apples in a valiant attempt to lure them down the steep mountain. Now Big Boy had carried one mouthful at a time, green alfalfa hay. My eyes filled with tears thinking about how this amazing dog had been providing protection and food for his friends. My heart overflowed with love and admiration for this dog that was winning a huge stride towards keeping his friends alive. Every fiber of his being focused on a goal that had to be filled with the hope of bringing his friends to being rescued. Big Boys persistence and his willingness to never give up has thus far prevailed!

There was a great sense of relief for me just thinking about Big Boys accomplishments. Now knowing for sure why he wouldn't come to me, and why he wasn't willing to leave the mountain for almost 3 months had now become so clear. Big Boy is one in a million, he is true to his heart. Big Boy is a soul that will never give up on what's right! He is a true hero, forsaking his own well being, risking his own life for his friends.

I'm in awe as I continue watching Big Boys friends eating a meal that had to have been a hard fight for Big Boy to deliver. His struggle with mother natures blanket of snow standing in his way, a meal not hand delivered, but mouth delivered. This much needed, nourishing meal to not just strengthen their bodies, but to provide the fuel they needed for body heat. Sustenance to provide them with the needed energy to win the battle of survival, hopefully leading them towards the biggest victory of all, rescue.

Big Boy didn't sit there waiting for his friends to finish eating. He knew he still had hard work ahead of him. He knew his friends were still in trouble with snow depths growing more and more. Big Boy was heading back down for another load of alfalfa hay.

It had taken me several hours to hike up to this viewpoint. It would take less time to get back down, following my trail up. But it would be getting late by the time I hiked back up the other side to fill Big Boys food dish, so I decided that it's time for me to do what Big Boy was doing, I headed down so I could hike in food for my friend. As I was hiking back down, my emotions were emotions of joy, no not just joy, I was elated! I am in awe of this majestic selfless dog! But I couldn't let this victory lead to a stale mate. This was a big victory, but it's going to take another victory to get all 4 of them off of that cliff.

I hiked down, and then back up the other side with my pack full of food for Big Boy. The sun was just about ready to set. While clearing away the snow to fill Big Boy's dish, I noticed that he had carried about half of that bale of alfalfa one mouthful at a time to his 3 friends. How much more can Big Boy do all by himself before Misses winter takes full control, sending down a heavy snowfall that will soon be too much for even a big powerful dog like Big Boy to withstand?

Chapter 41

The next morning after another snow storm overnight, the snow plows are out, concentrating their snow removal efforts here in the valley to clear off the roads to schools, hospitals, businesses and the roads going into residential areas. Their jobs were all about keeping everyone safe.

Bear Lake Valley was now covered with about 2 feet of snow. It snowed just over 23 inches in a single night. It's a lot of snow, so I get my snowblower out to clear the snow away from my driveway. My snowblower is 24 inches high where snow enters. It's all it could do to even move forward without backing it up, then ramming it forward.

As I'm removing the snow from my driveway, I'm thinking about what the snow depth must be up on the mountain. Big Boy was located about 2,000 feet in altitude higher than where I lived. I'm pretty sure if Big Boy has been keeping his trail well traveled, packing it with every pass, he might still be able to get to his food dish, and to the food for his friends. If he hasn't been using his trail, it could be too deep for him to be able to get any more supplies.

I load up more dog food preparing to head up the mountain for my daily trip to take supplies to Big Boy and his friends, praying that the road up the canyon has been cleared.

The snow is still falling after I finish snow blowing. I put my truck in 4 wheel drive, I pull forward and then back again to get enough of the snow underneath the truck packed down to where I could get enough momentum to be able to back up onto the highway. Thankfully, the snow plows had been working, coming by my house every hour or so all night long. I hadn't seen any snow plows in a couple hours. I'm hoping they have moved up, working hard at cleaning the road in heading up to Logan canyon. If they haven't gotten it cleared, my truck even in 4 wheel drive with new tires probably won't make it to where I can get Big Boy his daily supplies.

As I head up the canyon, I see that the road has been cleared! As I drove, I was thinking that it should have been a big relief to finally have seen the reason that Big Boy was on the mountain, having now seen Big Boys friends. But instead, this knowledge has put more weight on my mind. This rescue mission isn't just about one living thing, it's about four living things now.

I make it up to my parking spot and shovel it out so that I am able to park far enough off the road. I rest a bit after shoveling before I start my hike up. I get up to Big Boy's food dish, it's empty, and about ¾ of the bale of hay is gone. A scattering of the alfalfa leaves along the trail that Big Boy uses is a stark contrast against the snow packed trail. The bright green of the alfalfa hay against the white snow a tribute to the living legend who is determined to make sure that his friends have the nutrition that they need to continue to survive.

His trail wasn't stomped down as much as I had hoped for, but it was enough to where it looked like he would still be able to use it for a few more days.

Not being positive how much longer he could keep his trail open, I decided to overfill his food dish. I also decided to bring up another bale of hay. My thoughts were if I leave more food than he can eat, and more hay than he can keep carrying back to his friends, Big Boy would use his trail more. Keeping it open longer to possibly have another chance at saving Big Boy and his 3 sheep who were not just sheep to Big Boy, they were his friends.

Chapter 42

I had canceled my guided goose hunting trips for this week. It just wasn't worth any amount of money to take any unnecessary chances on someone getting hurt while traveling up here to Bear Lake Utah. There were already so many accidents down here low in Bear Lake valley, with even more going over through Logan Canyon. It's just not a very good time for any kind of travels right now. It's storming right now, with more storms lining up, heading this way all week long.

I had a whole week off from guiding, there was so many things that needed to be done around my old store to prepare it for wintertime that was already here with a lot more snow and cold to come.

While deciding what to do first, my mind was wondering again; Maybe there's a pathway down off that cliff that Big Boy hasn't discovered yet. Maybe there's a way to come in from the backside of this mountain. There's a canyon almost connecting to where Big Boys friends were stranded. With all of the snow now covering the area, there's a good chance that a snow cat or snowmobile could come over the top of the mountain, then down, running or side hilling on top of the snow just far enough from the steep cliffs to get close to where a rescue attempt could take place.

Getting my mind back to what I needed to do, I decided to drain and then pour antifreeze in all of my downstairs water pipes that ran throughout my store. The goal is to prevent the water pipes from freezing, which was my biggest concern. When water freezes it expands with great force or pressure, breaking water pipes, leaving you with not only no water, but with a lot of damage to your property. Broken pipes are no fun to fix, especially in old cinder block buildings like this one. A lot of pipes run right through the cinder blocks, when they break you've got to first find the broken pipe, then break away what compares to concrete to fix them. I had all my pipes drained and filled with antifreeze, then decided that was enough for today.

While draining the pipes, I found my snowshoes. My thinking was I'll hike back up that mountain across from where Big Boy was where I could take a closer look for a passageway coming over from the top to get him out of there. One concern facing me was a fear that the snow had filled in over the top of rocks, trees or anything else that would not only cause treacherous hiking, but the instability of the snow could cause an avalanche that would pick up debris on it's way down that mountain. Northern Utah has so many avalanches every winter, they claim many peoples lives each year. Utah has special guns that fire explosive charges into high risk places that safely discharges avalanches before they are triggered naturally, or by humans while they're recreating in back country areas. If an avalanche got triggered while I was hiking, or while Big Boy and his friends were stranded on that cliff, it could surely be an end to all.

Chapter 43

T he next morning I gathered together food for Big Boy, some treats for him of course, and loaded them into my truck. I have a couple bales of alfalfa hay left in the back of my truck for Big Boy's friends. For myself, I loaded my snowshoes and poles, water canteen, emergency fire starter, winter coat, hat, gloves, hand warmers and some high calorie snacks. After loading up the truck, I was off, heading for a fuel fill up before I headed up the mountain for my big hike.

I figured that my hike would most likely take most of the day. I was going to have to hike in mountainous terrain through at least 5 feet of snow, well aware that the wind could also have drifted the snow to twice that depth. Another danger was that the snow and snow drifts would be covering numerous unseen obstacles.

After my fuel fill up, I headed up the mountain road into a winter wonderland filled with both beauty and danger. The snow covered landscape was glistening like billions of tiny sparkling diamonds, so beautiful but also a sure sign of the frigid cold temperature.

I arrive at my parking place and dress in my winter wear. I load my binoculars, water, emergency fire starter and the high calorie snacks into my small hiking pack. Lastly, I don my snow shoes and I'm off.

My snowshoes keep me on top of the powdery snow, but if you've ever hiked in snowshoes, then you know it's not easy even on level ground. My ascent is slow and deliberate, using my poles to probe as well as steady me as I trudge up to my desired viewpoint.

When I finally arrive at my destination, I'm pretty exhausted. After resting a bit, I retrieve my binoculars from my pack. I carefully scan the opposite hillside for any possible route where it would be possible to come in from behind where Big Boy is located. To my surprise, I believe that my hunch was right! It looked like with very careful planning, it may be possible to come in from the opposite side of Big Boy's mountain, making it a possibility to get close enough to try a rescue.

Only one problem now, I don't have a snowmobile or snow cat to pull this whole rescue idea off. There's just no way possible to snowshoe in that great of a distance. Then, what would I do even if I could snowshoe in there? My disappointment in not having a snowmobile, or other way to get into where Big Boy and his friends were stranded tore at my heart. My negative thoughts making me think that this seemed to be another dead end. Frustration was setting in to a point of giving up.

I descend the mountain, back to my truck. After taking a break, hydrating and eating some snacks, I empty my backpack and load it up with Big Boy's food, leaving my hands free to carry the bale of hay. I begin taking Big Boys food and another bale of hay up to where I've been leaving them. Sundown is only about an hour away, I've got to finish getting the food up there before dark. I'm exhausted by the time I reach Big Boy's food dish. All the hay that I had left was gone, so I'm glad that I brought up another bale. I clean the snow out and fill Big Boys food dish, cut the strings on the bale of hay and sit down. I can only take a brief rest before I've got to get back down to my truck before dark. As I sit there, I can hear the wind howling, a lonely, desperate sound that's reflecting my current feelings. Luckily, giving up isn't a word in my vocabulary. There's no such thing as giving up on my friend Big Boy. I take a deep determined breath of the cold evening air, and head back down to my truck.

The roads are icy where packed patches of snow cover the surface as I drive home. The wind had blown snow across several areas making the drive home slower than normal. I finally get off the mountain safely and back home. I spend another sleepless night trying to figure out how I'm going to pull off this rescue.

Chapter 44

The next morning I fill Big Boys food dish, there's not much of the hay left, Big Boy was on his trail again, hauling the food to his friends. By now, there was no way to see him once he entered his pathway. The snow was so deep it had formed walls on both sides. Big Boy would disappear when he entered it, then reappear when he came out of it.

As I sit on this cold and snowy mountain, large snowflakes falling silently, I stare at my friends food dish talking to myself; 'Our time grows even shorter my friend. There's been added dangers that are all betting against getting you and your friends out of here. Our time grows short, we've got to make a move right now my friend. I have a lot to say to you Big Boy, I want to hear what you have to say to me, my heart is breaking for you and for your 3 friends, but there is no way for us to communicate. No way for me to make you understand that I want to get you home safe Big Boy.

Big Boy we've gone through a lot so far. It's going to get worse soon, it's going to get bad if we don't get all of you out of here soon.'

I hike back down to my truck and make the drive back home, barely making it back home without going off the road as I had slid sideways several times on the steep downhill part of the canyon road. I also had to bust through some large snowdrifts that were blocking the road. Misses winter was lining up her deep snow with her friend Mister wind. They both were getting together for a few days. When Misses winter and Mister wind get together, they both try to impress each other with their powerful forces of nature. Misses winter will show off by bringing her heavy snow to the plate. She works extra hard when showing off, sending sometimes several feet of snow in just one single storm. To retaliate, Mister wind huffs, puffs, then blows with all of his might sending powerful winds that displace Misses winters snow. When these two get together, it really causes problems for every living thing. It fills in all nooks and crannies, pathways or places with any bare and open area. Another thing that Mister wind does when he blows heavy wind, is he blows any leaves, berries or forage foods to the ground. Then Misses winter covers it up with snow, removing some of the last winter food for the wild animals to eat to survive through their time of need. Basically, Misses winter and Mister wind cause a lot of trouble when they spend time together. I'm kind of wishing they weren't such good friends, always competing to see who was strongest with their natural powers.

Chapter 45

Overnight there was no such thing as sleep. Actually during this whole rescue attempt, I had almost forgotten what a good nights sleep was. Mister wind had been blowing hard all night long at my house. I park my truck next to a vacant property that's about 3 feet higher than my property. When Mister wind blows from that direction, he blows snow up against my house and my truck. When I went out to my truck in the morning, it was drifted in with deep snow. Again the snowblower came out, and I tackle the task of clearing my drive. I had to use a shovel on the 4-5 foot snowdrifts that had built up in front, behind and all along the entire side of my crew cab truck. I put the truck in 4 wheel drive, rocking backwards, then forwards several times until I could bust free from the snow that the wind had packed underneath the truck where I was unable to reach to remove it. Finally my truck was free, and I was in an area that I had cleared out. I put chains on every tire, wanting to ensure that I was doing all that I could to be able to make it up to Big Boy and his friends. I finally made it out onto the road to go see how bad it was up where Big Boy was stranded.

The snow plows had tried to keep up with the heavy snow with very little success. Before I even reached the canyon road, there were two 18 wheel trucks stuck off the side of the road where they had slid off. There was even a snow plow that was completely sideways and sitting off of the road in a deep snow bank. Cars were scattered along the road, especially on the curves where they had hit ice and slid off. At the entrance of Logan Canyon, the flashing road sign indicated that only 4 wheel drive trucks, or cars with chains on their tires were allowed to enter. I had both the 4 wheel drive and chains. It took me almost 2 hours to get to my parking spot, then another hour digging a spot out to park safely.

As I was putting on my snow shoes, I could hear Big Boy. His howls were pitiful, he sounded like he was in trouble. With tears streaming down my face, I hurried up the mountain to get to Big Boys food spot, hoping that he was there, or within sight on his trail. I was frantically climbing. Tripping over my snowshoes I fell, loosing one of my gloves. I fell several more times, my glove-less hand grabbing a hold on brush and rocks as I climbed. Out of breath, and with a scraped and bloody hand, I reached his food dish.

I could hear Big Boy very clearly now, he was somewhere close by, but nowhere in sight. He's got to be close. I could tell that he was on his trail, and that he was struggling, his voice reflected his deep breathing. The kind of breathing you would hear coming from a professional athlete at the end of his long endurance race. His huffing reminded me of a lineman blasting forward, trying to tackle the quarterback. Big Boy was grunting with loud whimpers in his voice. Stopping occasionally to let out one of his pitiful howls and catch his breath. I pictured Big Boy doing what I had to do to get my truck unstuck early this morning. He was ramming forward trying to clear his trail that led toward me and his food. He knew that I was standing at his food dish awaiting his arrival.

I could now see him, far up on the trail. Big Boys head would pop up above snow level, then he would fall backwards, presumably onto his back.

This went on for what seemed to me to be hours, until Big Boys strength was exhausted. His voice grew weak, now just small whimpers, with no more grunts of charging hard while he blasted forward. I stood as if frozen, watching him. With our eyes locked, Big Boy sat quietly on his trail. A look of despair in his eyes, tears streaming down my face and into my beard where they froze solid. We held each others eyes for a few minutes, then my friend turned, his head down in defeat as he headed back up his trail toward his friends.

Chapter 46

In a panic, I rushed forward, up the way that Big Boys trail had been before this big snow storm. With the snow covering the big boulders, I was able to get to where I was underneath the cliff where Big Boy and his friends were stranded. Luckily my my snowshoes were keeping me on top, allowing me to get closer to Big Boys friends than I'd ever been. On the steep slope up above me I could see the trail that Big Boy had been able to make in his attempt to reach me and his food dish. He had made it barely into where the wind had drifted the snow into a deep wave that I guessed was at least 10 feet deep. The drift continued down the slope and was even deeper, several feet deeper just ahead of me. Between the steepness and the huge snow drift, it was impossible for me to try to climb any further. Only having dog food with me, there was no way that I could leave food here on top of the snow for Big Boy. Even if I did, he may not be able to push through enough snow to reach it.

I stood there, trying to think of how to get food to Big Boy. Maybe if I could mold some raw ground beef into a ball. Fashioning it like a snowball, it would be possible for me to throw it up where Big Boy could get to it?

Still in a panic, I head back to my truck, then home, driving too fast on the snow packed road. I'm anxious and desperate to get some hamburger. My plan is to get the meat, and head right back up with the meat snowballs. Hoping that I can throw them up on top of the cliff where my friend could reach them.

Chapter 47

I get home and rush to my freezer. All that I had in my freezer were flat, frozen deer burgers. In my mind I formulated a plan. I figured I'd chop them up into small flat pieces, and throw them, flying them like a Frisbee. Hoping that if they didn't reach far enough, they would skip like a rock does on the surface of water. Using a few skips if needed to cover the distance to reach Big Boy.

My burgers in hand, I hit the road. Not in as much of a state of panic, I notice that the road is now clear from drifting snow. Most of the trucks and cars had been pulled out, back up on the road to safety, letting everyone be on their way.

I get back up to my parking spot and hike back up where I can, I'm hoping, to be able to throw the meat up to Big Boy. I hike up as far as I can, just as I had done a few hours ago. Big Boy had rested up for the few hours that I had been gone to get the burger. When he saw me, he barked a few times with his familiar greeting, although his barks weren't strong or loud anymore. But at least he was still barking. My hopes were still high at this point. When Big Boy grows silent with no barks anymore, then it's going to possibly be over for all of them. It's so critical that Big Boy eats to help keep him warm at night. There weren't any more worries about Big Boy having to protect his friends, there's no way now that wolves or coyotes could travel if they were still up here in the high country. If they were up this high, they would be facing everything that Big Boy is facing. They'd be stranded in a small area, not being able to move far.

As I stood there catching my breath after my hike up, I was taking notice of the area. It didn't look like there was very much snow under the trees, the small group of animals had tromped it down. Leading out from the trees was a trail heading to the edge of a steep cliff. The wind had blown the snow off of the edge of this cliff, it was right down to the bare shale rock. Big Boy was standing like a beautiful statue at the edge of the shale rock where the giant drift started. He was such a magnificent sight, he stood so proudly, like a monarch standing watch over his domain.

Getting my stance set, I begin throwing the meat like a Frisbee up towards where Big Boy is standing. The chunks of meat were a lot harder to throw than I had thought they would be. Trying to wing this frozen meat wasn't working very well. It was so hard to throw it with any accuracy. As I threw the meat, Big Boy stood, waiting for a perfectly placed shot to reach him. There was over 10 feet of deep, blown snow across a hundred foot area between me and Big Boy. Snow so deep that it was a death trap if Big Boy got stuck in it.

A few pieces of the flat meat were making it almost far enough, almost to the area where Big Boy had pushed his way through the snow drift a few hours ago. The wind had already almost completely filled in the trail that he had tried to make, but maybe he could get through it again to get to the meat.

Big Boy had to be hungry, but he knew better than to try to get to the meat that I was throwing for him that was falling way short. His attempt to get through the drift a few hours ago had failed, so I'm sure that he was weary of trying to attempt going through the drift again. My hopes for being able to throw these flat pieces of ground deer meat up to my friend were quickly dashed. As I said, I had hoped that maybe they would skip like a rock did on top of the water, skipping on the top of the snow until coming to a stop, reaching to where it would be easy for Big Boy to retrieve them. 3 out of a dozen of them made it up quite a ways, but just not far enough. Even if Big Boy could get to them, the 3 of them really wouldn't be much more than a snack for him. Throwing his meat like a Frisbee just isn't going to work. It's basically been a waste of my food for Big Boy. And a waste of my food that I also counted on to get through the winter.

There's got to be a better way to throw food, hitting the bullseye. After my hikes and my failed attempt to throw food for Big Boy, I was getting hungry too. Us humans are so blessed to have a pantry, freezer, fridge, or just being able to stop into a store or restaurant, getting pretty much what ever our bellies are hungry for, at any time that we want it.

Chapter 48

Giving up, I hike back down to my truck. As I head off of the mountain, my trucks warning light came on, letting me know it was time to fill up with gas. By the time that I get back to town, its pretty late, I'm exhausted after my trying day, so I know that I'm not going to feel like cooking anything for my dinner when I get home.

I stopped at the first gas station/convenience store, filling up my tank, then getting a gut bomb dinner of jalapeno corn dogs. The corn dogs were pretty cheap and would fill my belly up. Instead if driving while eating them, I sat outside of the store eating them. As I ate, I looked at the corn dogs, my mind wondering, thinking that if by pulling out this stick from a corn dog, it would become like a small football. I'll bet I can throw these corn dogs with way better success than flat frozen meat up onto Big Boys cliff! It's worth a try, and they were a lot more affordable than red meat. With the corn and fat content they were not only full of calories, but a big plus was that Big Boy might really like them! Corn dogs are pretty dang good.

I ran back into the store, buying the 6 corn dogs that were out and available for me to purchase. I'd leave early in the morning before this store was open or had corn dogs out for sale, so I thought I'd better buy them now. I figured that it was cold enough just leaving them in my truck overnight, they would still be fine until morning.

Again...It was so hard to sleep that night thinking about launching this new plan of throwing corn dogs like a football up to my friend Big Boy stranded on that cliff. At this point, there wasn't anything I could do to get his friends more food. My hopes were that Big Boy had carried enough alfalfa hay up to them to last them a little while, at least adding a bit to their fat stores, until we could come up with a plan to get them all out of there before they froze or starved to death. Speaking for myself, it would be a terrible way to die, freezing or starving to death. But both of them put together would be a horrific way to go. My determination still held strong, there's just no way I'm letting this happen.

I'm the type person that if they're your friends, and we are friends, then they are my friends too. So really, it's not just my friend Big Boy up there, it's 4 of my friends that need help being rescued.

Chapter 49

I'm up early and headed up the canyon with the corn dogs. I hiked up again in my snow shoes, stick-less corn dogs stuffed in my coat pockets. I get there and there was Big Boy sitting at the edge of the cliff/snowdrift, his long pearly white hair wavering in the wind. His chin held high, his nose full of scents traveling through this high mountain range. Big Boy was just as beautiful as he has always been. I wondered if one of those scents he was sniffing was his smells of home. If I'm right about who his owner is, he basically lied about Big Boy being his dog in order to save his own skin from coming up against possible animal cruelty charges and/or charges for abandoning such a precious soul like Big Boy. If I'm right, Big Boy's home wasn't that far away. If Big Boy would have abandoned his friends months ago like his owner had done to him, he could have cut through this mountain range and would have been safe at home in just a few days. By way of a birds flight in a straight line, his home was only about 20 miles away. It would have been a cinch for such a powerful dog to cover that much ground without even breaking a sweat.

Big Boy was nothing like his owner, this dog had too much integrity. Big Boy was driven by his heart to do without question what is right. In this case, his heart stood with his friends until his heart didn't beat anymore, or until all 4 of them got home safe.

Chapter 50

It was time to try my football skills out, throwing like a wide receiver these 6 tasty corn dogs. With Big Boy waiting to make a game winning catch. I'm sure he would make that catch, if I could make a good throw! Big Boy was waiting patiently, and fully alert. He knew I had brought him food, even if he hadn't seen it yet. Food to fill his belly and stave off what had to be a painful hunger by now.

'Are you ready Big Boy? Get ready Boy, keep your eyes on the ball Big Boy. Here it comes Big Boy. You got this Big Boy!' I hollered up to my friend.

Taking aim, rearing back, I let the first corn dog fly. It flew straight, with kind of a wobble to it, flying above the snowdrift, heading right inline for Bog Boy.

Wow! I have a better throwing arm than I thought! It went right over Big Boys head, landing about 20 feet behind him. Big Boy had already turned his body, side stepping backwards and taking off at a trot following the corn dog as it flew through the air. As the corn dog hit, Big Boy was right there scooping it up before it even had a chance to bounce. Big Boy had gotten it! Whoo Hoo!!!

Being excited, I had no delay in launching number 2 on it's way. This corn dog flew true, striking it's target, right next to Big Boy. 3, 4 and 5 were on their way, all hitting right on the bullseye! One to go, so I reared back letting number 6 go.

Number 6 flew a little wild, it was just a little off course. Striking like a lawn dart, it burrowed down through a deep snow bank just off to the side of Big Boy. My friend disappeared for only a few short seconds, returning to stand prouder than proud with a corn dog hanging out of the side of his mouth. It was like Big Boy was showing me not only that he had gotten his corn dog, it was as if he was saying 'thank you.' Big Boy was showing his gratitude in his own way.

Wishing there were more corn dogs to throw up to Big Boy, but knowing that they were gone, we both turned heading away from each other. Just wishing we would see each other again sooner than later. This was another successful plan that had come together. So far there hasn't been a lot of plans come together. But every time one did, it was a huge step towards our plan of somehow getting Big Boy and his friends back home.

It was storming on my way home. Snow packed roads made what's normally a short trip turn into a pretty long trip. On my way home I stopped to buy more corn dogs. They had 9 of them, I wished there were more but it would be 3 more than what Big Boy had gotten today. If my aim held true tomorrow like it did today, Big Boy would have a big meal coming his way.

Chapter 51

M ister wind and Misses snow must have had enough of each others company. Now it was all Misses snow, she was showing off her powers again as she was bringing down a record snowstorm in Northern Utah. She had dropped almost 70 inches of snow high up in the mountains. It was great for ski resorts, but not so good for my friends still stranded on that steep cliff.

This whole rescue attempt had been now going for 3 months. It all started when I was just driving over Logan Canyon to Logan City Utah to get supplies. Never would I have thought that single day would turn into 3 a month commitment. Returning back up Logan Canyon almost every single day to try to rescue, at that time, a dog that I didn't even know. But now, that dog named Big Boy has become important to me. Big Boy has become my lifetime friend.

Chapter 52

Once again, here I am returning to try to launch some more corn dogs. First again, making the drive with chains on all 4 tires, then taking over an hour to dig through several feet of snow that the snow plows had pushed into where I parked my truck safely from oncoming traffic. I had brought my dogs with me today, knowing there was no chance I'd be taking Big Boy in my truck. Leaving my dogs safe in my truck, I put my snowshoes on and headed up.

First I had to climb a huge bank of snow that had been stacked up by the snow plows. Going up, the snow was really deep, I was glad to have my snowshoes to keep me on top of the snow. It took awhile longer to make the trek up the mountain with the added snow. Today, there was no Big Boy standing so beautiful with his pearly long white hair blowing in the wind.

'Here Big Boy, here Big Boy, here Big Boy. Come on Big Boy, where are you Big boy? I got your corn dogs Big Boy. Here Big Boy.'

There still was no Big Boy. I got out my binoculars, looking upwards. Looking for any trails or imprints that would let me know Big Boy was still here. There was no sign of life anywhere. There was so much snow it had smoothed everything out, making it hard to identify even the shale area where Big Boy had stood yesterday. The deep snow smoothed off the rock cliffs, totally covering the berry bushes and even the smaller trees.

There wasn't much that could be done right now except stay positive about this situation.

I decided to go ahead and throw these 9 corn dogs up to where Big Boy had caught them yesterday. My aim held true, all 9 corn dogs landed pretty close together, within just a few feet of where Big Boy had caught them yesterday.

There wasn't anything pressing me, or things that needed to be done. So when I got back down to my truck, my dogs and I just sat there, the windows part way down, listening and watching for any movement up on this mountain.

Wanting to turn on my radio to listen to some music that would help soothe my mind, helping to calm me down. I decided that wasn't such a good idea, it would be hard to hear a bark or noise from Big Boy with any music or distractions going on. So we sat there quietly, with my truck window down, one hour went by, then 2 or 3. After a few more hours, my gas was just about gone. There was just enough left to ensure that we got home safely, with just a small amount of gas left in case we got in any trouble on our way.

Chapter 53

My heart is broken, I am full of despair having known for the last 3 months that if Big Boy wasn't down off that mountain by this time of year, it wouldn't have a happy ending.

When I watch a movie where there's not a happy ending, it's for sure a movie I'm not going to ever watch again, I'm definitely not going to pass that movie on, or recommend it to other people. For me, it was like this real life movie that was playing out for me now. But this movie was real, there's no high paid actors in this movie. No props, no fake deaths, no cuts saying 'cut, let's redo this scene.' Everything here right now is life, it's real life and real things. Real conditions that will simply determine if life will continue, or life will cease to be. No one knew about this movie but me. No one has been told yet.

I hadn't shared this movie with anyone because I was still believing there would be a happy ending. There are 5 actors in this real life movie who aren't getting paid. 4 of them involved in a real possibility of paying not in money, but with their lives. No one but me knew about this movie of a real life magical dog, a dog that had done his best to try to overcome this deck of cards that had been stacked against him, a dog named Big Boy who was getting cheated by someone who should in good conscience, be there to protect him throughout his life, ensuring a happy ending for him. This person was his owner. I call him a schmuck who doesn't deserve to own a dog. To me, when the cards are stacked against you from someone that's cheating, yet you overcome it, turning the tide on them, still coming out with a win, it's even a sweeter, happier ending. I must make this story end with the sweet, happy ending. But how?

Chapter 54

It was a clear night. Finding myself laying in bed staring out my window, looking up into thousands of shining stars. Some stars big, some small. I imagined stars just coming to life so excited to be alive, sharing their rays of brightness for many years to come. Some stars shined brighter than others, some stars had shined themselves out, becoming shooting stars with one last burst of energy shining even brighter than their light had shone their very first day. These stars were for me wishing stars. I had always tried to make a positive wish on every shooting stars last journey of shining bright as it flies through a clear and beautiful night sky. If my wish came true, it was a way of that shooting star living on for many more years to come. Normally there's a separate wish for each shooting star, but on this clear freezing cold night, every wish was the same. They all were wishes that my friends would just hold on. Please just hold on you guys. Please shooting stars make my dreams come true. Please stars, I've always believed in you. Please shooting stars, just please make just this one dream come true.

It was morning now and all the beautiful shining stars were gone. But they would return next time the night sky was clear and dark blue. If my friends weren't safe by the next clear night sky, I would be waiting to wish upon a star again.

Temperatures had dropped into sub zero. It was -22 as I headed back to my friends last location. Stopping on my way to pick up more corn dogs and filling up my tank with gas. I'm here now, sitting quietly again scanning for any signs of life. There was just nothing that could live here this time of year. Thinking about things that might be here, my thoughts changed to Heavenly Father in His master plan of all His creatures. Really, there was life here, there were birds and there were creatures like bears who would find a den, cave or cavern that would keep them dry and warm while they slept all winter long. Like all those shining stars, they would wait until conditions were right, then appear again to live and enjoy their lives. I'd sat here all day long, besides some birds, there wasn't any other life that was visible to see with your naked eyes. There was no life to see on this snow covered mountain. All life seemed to be gone. Darkness would be upon me soon. My voice had gone hoarse from yelling for Big Boy all day long with no answers from him. Big Boy had to still be here, he just had to be! There was nowhere else he could be. Big Boy was a purebred Great Pyrenees, they're a breed that's legendary for withstanding places just like this, in these same conditions. Doing this same thing of sticking by their friends sides while protecting them. Great Pyrenees are kings of any mountain. These kinds of kings like Big Boy stood strong, they are objects of history. Withstanding all tests of time.

Big Boy is still here, he's here even though he hasn't spoken or greeted me in 2 days. He's here. His presence was so strong. It's like his presence is inside of me, urging me not to give up, I just know that Big Boy is still alive. Deciding to go with this kind of bizarre feeling that had become like a silent language between true friends, my hopes were re sparked by this feeling deep inside my heart. Big Boy is here. True friends never abandon each other in times of need. Sometimes one friend just steps up to the plate, waiting for his friend to join in.

Chapter 55

I headed back home to feed my own dogs, check up on them and fill their food dishes. I just can't stand this pain, I'm grabbing my sleeping bag and filling up my truck with gas. I have to go back up the mountain, I can't shake my hearts feelings that Big Boy was still there. I'd leave my truck running with it's heater on low to stay overnight, close to Big Boy.

I sat there in my truck on the mountain, there were no shining stars to watch while making more wishes on them. It's cloudy with just a soft breeze. Temperatures were still close to -20.

I laid down across the seat, bundled up in my sleeping bag, I'm thinking of times when I'd been lost. Not just the times lost in the wilderness, eventually finding my way, but times throughout my life when I felt lost. Times that I felt my life had no purpose or meaning. Times I'd about given up on myself. It's pitch black outside with no landmarks. Now my thoughts have drifted to thinking of all my years guiding fishermen on the Pacific ocean, trying to squeeze in just a few more minutes of fishing before it's too dark to get home.

There were several times where just spending those few extra minutes trying to catch one last fish, turned into the darkness of night, darkness being upon us with no guiding lights in sight to help bring us home. I remember trying to find my way far enough to spot that one shining light that stands alone all by itself. That light has guided uncountable people to safety. That light is a lighthouse put there to guide boats to safety on nights like this one. Thinking about that life saving lighthouse, I turn on my truck lights, hoping to just maybe let Big Boy know his friend is still nearby. I still had hope, I was hoping if Big Boy could see even a glimpse of my truck lights, it would give him hope too.

Throughout the night, I'd get up turning off my truck and sit quietly just listening for any noise that sounded out of place. A few times I woke up, thinking Big Boy was barking. Barks of joy 'wooooof wooooof wooooooof.' Here I come! They were big drawn out barks like when we first met. Over this last 3 months, I'd gotten to know most every kind of sound of Big Boy's barks. He had a pretty big vocabulary. Big Boy was always speaking through different tones in his voice. Sleep took over for a few hours.

I woke up just as Mister sunshine broke over the ridge with his rays of light. It was bitter cold, -32 degrees outside. It's what I've always called 'Arctic' outside. When it's arctic outside, it just takes the fun out of trying to enjoy being or doing anything outdoors. It's just plain arctic, it's too cold.

Was I still dreaming? Am I really here right now? Are my ears being controlled by my mind, wanting so badly to hear Big Boy's voice? I hear him, I'm not sleeping or still dreaming! I hear Big Boy!

Big Boy wasn't barking, Big Boy's voice sounded muffled. It was strong, but muffled, there wasn't really even a bark. 'Big Boy, here Big Boy, here Boy! Big Boy come on Big Boy!' My voice was pretty much gone from the last 2 days of yelling, almost screaming for Big Boy to come.

His voice was more like he was crying ' wa oooooo rooooooooo wa ooooooooo rooooooo rooooooooo.' His cries had me feeling my friends pain, huge tears were streaming down my face, choking sobs of both sorrow and joy fill my chest, causing my throat to constrict. I'm not able to yell anymore because of the strong emotion I am feeling right now at finally hearing Big Boy. You know when you get really upset, or are crying when you kind of huff? Your cries get broken up with emotions breaking the length of your cries. Then there's a huff in between? Myself and my friend were both huffing in between our cries.

After gaining my composure, my inner heart spoke to me saying 'You need to stay strong for not only yourself Jimmy, you're friends are in a time of need. All 4 of them need you now, right now, there wouldn't be a later time, it would be too late. Your time is right now.'

I stopped my cries, trying to send a subliminal message to Big Boy.

'It's just you and me Big Boy, it's you and me that needs to stay strong right now, it's up to you and me Big Boy. We need to stay strong for our friends.'

I knew that Big Boy's cries weren't from physical pain. He was a warrior. Warriors never feel pain from an injury. Warriors welcome injuries, it makes them heal up even stronger than before. Warriors need to learn to lean on Gods strength. Warriors need to remember that not a sparrow falls without God knowing, and as their creator, He truly cares that they have fallen.

Big Boy's cries weren't from hunger. Big Boy didn't ever complain. During Big Boy's life of doing his job of protecting his friends, he had felt hunger. Big Boy faced hunger with being grateful for his next meal.

Big Boy wasn't crying from being cold. Heavenly Father created Big Boy's kind to have the means to protect him from any cold conditions set forth to him to simply overcome.

Big Boy's crying for his friends. He is crying because he had done his very best to stick by his friends sides, protecting them from harm and from hunger to the best of his ability. Big Boy isn't used to any form of defeat. He's never been defeated before in his life in anything.

Big Boys cries come from thinking he failed his friends by letting them down. He's thinking about something that's not true. There's no truth to his thinking right now. Big Boy had done everything in his power to save his friends. His desire has always been to bring all 3 of them home safely. Big Boy doesn't realize there's no controlling the uncontrollable. If Big Boy had chose to be selfish, he could have left his 3 friends at any time, saving himself. Big Boy could be home right now, laying in a bed of fresh straw with a full food dish just feet away. Being nice and warm, with a full belly. Just relaxing with no worries in his world. But through it all, Big Boys choice was to do the right thing, the selfless thing, which makes him a legend. Big Boy hasn't failed anyone.

I knew that I had been crying for the same reasons that Big Boy was. My thoughts were exactly in line with his, thoughts of thinking that I'd let my friends down. If myself and Big Boy are as much the same as I think we are, his heart will come forth like mine did. Snapping him out from his cries of letting his friends down. Snap out of this mindset

Big Boy, snap out of it! You're stronger than me Big Boy, if I can do it, you can too.

Big Boy cried for what seemed to be an eternity. His last cries grew weak. Big Boys voice had faded away into a the silence of a barren snow covered cliffy mountain with no life apparent on it's surface.

Chapter 56

I needed help. I left home as a young boy, making my way through life, never once asking for help. My thoughts went back to this moment. Maybe part of Big Boys cries were sucking up his pride. Maybe Big Boy was crying for help.

One thing that bonds true friends, true friends for life, is when one, and then the other is able to swallow their pride, just let that pride go, and ask for a helping hand.

Another thing about true friends, is learning from each other. Never be too proud to know we all don't know everything. We can learn from each other. Learning just helps us all be better people. Big Boy just taught me a valuable life lesson. I'm positive now that part of Big Boys cries were cries for help. He had let go of his pride.

Taking my true friends life lesson, my pride was getting set aside for now. I'm sure it will come back soon, but for now my pride would have to take a back seat.

There's no phone service this high up in this mountain range. With my pride set aside now, and thinking how foolish I've been throughout my life letting pride be such a big thing. At some points in all of our lives, we're all needing help. We all need that pride less faith in a loving God. We all need to let go of our pride and rely on help from our friends.

I'm heading off the mountain to where I have cell service. Slowing myself down, I'm driving way too fast to get my other true friends help. Big Boy just made me grow in life. Now in a hurry to ask for help, for my very first time.

This felt good. This feeling was new to me, but it just felt right. This new feeling felt good.

Even though my friends were still back there behind me now, there was an overwhelming feeling of calm.

I called my friend as soon as my phone got service. My friend was a lot older than me, I looked up to him in so many ways. With sobs and tears I tried to tell him my story over the phone. He asked me to come to his house and tell him all about these last 3 months, I'm sure that he was having a hard time trying to understand me on the phone in my emotional condition. I drove to my friends house. After telling my friend, his response was, 'Why didn't you tell me this 3 months ago? I'd have been right there helping you Jimmy. Everyone was wondering why you drove up the canyon every morning and sometimes at night. We all thought you had met a girl in Logan, not wanting to fill us all in on details. Is this where you've been going all this time? Jimmy, this is an easy problem to solve. You're not the only one who loves dogs. We all do, we all love animals especially dogs. Go public with this Jimmy. Don't you have a good friend that writes for the newspaper in Logan? It's simple, let the world know about this dog you named Big Boy! Then, be prepared for what's going to happen. Do it now, do it right now Jimmy.'

Chapter 57

I left my friends house, and pull over onto the side of the road. While sitting in my truck, I call my friend that was an editor for the newspaper in Logan City. I knew that he also ran online articles that would reach places that his newspaper didn't reach. I barely started telling my friend about Big boy when he stopped me and said, 'Jimmy there's no time for your story. Time is critical right now, just tell me where up Logan Canyon this is happening. I'll meet you there, I'm walking to my truck right this second. I'll be there meeting you within the hour.'

We met up where Big Boy was. My friend wrote down the location, along with parts of my story. He was short in his stay, telling me 'don't worry, when this dog story comes out first thing tomorrow morning, all hell is going to break loose! Big Boy and his friends are going to be okay Jimmy, mark my words. Your friends will be okay.'

My newspaper friend left, I sat there in my truck anxious, and hopeful that I'd done the right thing. Deciding to stay another night in my truck, wanting to be up as close to Big Boy as I could be, my thoughts went to thinking of not just my 4 friends stranded on this mountain. My thoughts had gone to how much I have been blessed in my life to have such amazing friends. Friends that are now stepping up, helping me to rescue my friends that have now become their friends as well.

I was excited for Big Boys story to hit the headlines in a pretty big newspaper. The newspaper would be available early the following morning. There are thousands of people that subscribe, people intent on keeping up with local and national news and current events.

I'd been sitting there in my truck for a couple of hours when search and rescue vehicles pulled off the road and parked right behind my truck. 3 men and 1 woman get out, I notice that all of them are dressed in snow pants with heavy winter coats on. All of them approach my truck as I watch them in my side mirror. As I watch them, I'm wondering if they are here about Big Boy, but how could they be?

Chapter 58

I didn't know at this time that my newspaper friend had zoomed back down Logan Canyon, getting into town and to his computer he had wasted no time. He had written Big Boys story, then he had uploaded it into the internet. I had no idea that Big Boys story had broke within an hour of my friends departure, hours before the newspaper had even come out! Big Boys story was already reaching tens of thousands of people throughout this whole country!

With weak shaking legs, I got out of my truck as the search and rescue team approached my door. 'Are you Jimmy? Is this where a dog named Big Boy needs our help to get him off of this mountain?' With shaking hands and tears in my eyes I reply, 'Yes, I'm Jimmy. And yes, Big Boy, a Great Pyrenees is stranded up on the mountain. He's been protecting 3 sheep that are up on the mountain with him. They are all stranded way up, almost to the top, surrounded by steep cliffs, deep snow, and large snow drifts. They are underneath some trees. They do not have access to food, they are all in serious trouble.

These search and rescue people get out several pairs of binoculars, they began scanning the mountain, looking for a way to come in to do a rescue. They came to the same conclusion that I had, the only possible way to get into where my friends were stranded, was to come in from Beaver Mountain Ski Resort. Beaver Mountain was about 10 miles behind where Big Boy was stranded.

One of the search and rescue team members said 'I think that we can, with ease, come down that ravine. Putting us just above Big Boy. Has Big Boy shown any aggression towards you? We might have to shoot him with a tranquilizer gun to ensure his safety, as well as our safety.' 'No,' I replied, 'Big Boy hasn't let me touch him, but he's been within just a few feet of me several times when he has come down for his food. Big Boy doesn't seem to be mean or aggressive at all. But it is his job to protect his sheep, a job he so obviously takes very seriously since he has refused to leave them. So you may need to tranquilize him for safety.'

With compassion in his eyes, and in his voice, the search and rescue member tells me, 'Jimmy thank you for bringing this to our attention, we're already getting rescue equipment ready to go. All of our people will be in Beaver Mountain ski resorts parking lot at daybreak. Don't worry Jimmy, we're going to do everything we can to get Big Boy and his friends safely off of this mountain. I have dogs of my own, and every time something like this happens, it upsets me greatly. It's not the dogs that I get upset at, it's the owners! People like that don't deserve to ever own such a precious animal. I'm sure if the authorities find out who's dog this is, that's obviously been abandoned, there could be some charges filed against them.'

Then the search and rescue team got back into their vehicles, and they left. Still standing there outside of my truck, I gaze up towards the heavens, with tears of joy now freezing in my beard, mingling with my tears of anguish from just a few minutes ago. Bowing my head, I'm giving my thanks and my praise to God, my Heavenly Father, and to His shooting stars for answering my prayers and granting my wishes. I now knew that God had been answering my prayers all along, He had kept Big Boy alive. He had opened my heart to care for a dog that I didn't even know. He had given me the means to buy and to bring the food. He had ensured that I had a 4 wheel drive truck. Right now it is so very, very clear to me how every single thing that we have comes from God. A knowing of this truth is inside of us all if you really take the time to think about it. Our very lives are not possible had He not created us, therefore every single thing that we have, that we think we own, has come from God. Nothing exists outside of His creation, absolutely nothing!

I am so humbled realizing that He had done it all, but because He has chosen to give us free will, He had left it up to me to reach out for help. It had been up to me the whole time, it had been up to me to set aside my pride, and to give others their chance to join me in caring for Gods creatures.

He was waiting for me to see, and to recognize that His hand is ever present in my life. It had been up to me to share the love of His only begotten Son, Jesus to others through mutual love for His creatures.

I was overwhelmed with the presence of His love.

Chapter 59

Within 30 minutes of the search and rescue vehicles leaving, the road in Logan Canyon was chaos. There were cars after cars coming up to where I was parked. There were people walking up and down the road yelling for Big Boy. One guy even brought one of those cone shaped speaker things. It didn't work very well, it was so freezing cold that every time he spoke into it there was just squelches that came out. This is so unbelievable! How many people are trying to help Big Boy?

I'm now a firm believer in the power of social media and the internet! WOW, I'm blown away. I wonder if Big Boy is up there watching and hearing all of this action going on? If he is, I hope he knows, we're coming to get him!

Chapter 60

Darkness was setting in. Temperatures were dropping. All traffic was gone now, it was just me, my dogs and my 4 friends left up here on this mountain. I couldn't help but feel that I was dreaming with my eyes wide open.

I'm praying for every ones safety in tomorrows rescue attempt. I'm thinking of what a spiritual journey this whole thing had been. For so many reasons I now see that all of this happened just as it was meant to happen. An unknown spiritual journey for me that began the day that I was just driving to Logan to get supplies, then seeing a stray dog in Logan Canyon, a spiritual adventure that had consumed me for over 3 months now, still not being over.

Morning felt like it would never come. With my windows cracked open, there were no sounds or noises. It was deathly calm and quiet. There were so many stars out this night. There wasn't much I could do, so I started counting stars. Some probably got counted several times over, but it occupied my mind. As I drifted off to sleep counting stars, I thought of my friend Al, he was always saying that we should count our lucky stars. Yes my friend, I need to always remember to count my lucky stars.

Chapter 61

While it was still dark, I drove to the Beaver Mountain parking lot. Mister sun was just about ready to stretch out while letting a big yawn, then get up to go do his work for another day of lighting a new day up with his brilliance.

When I got there, the parking lot was packed with all kinds of people. People had set up pavilions with chairs under them. There were people unloading snow machines, warming them up, getting ready to go. Other people were cooking food and making hot drinks for everyone. Search and rescue had brought a big enclosed trailer to hopefully transport Big Boy with his friends.

There were police, game wardens, photographers, reporters, basically that whole parking lot was full of people that were there because of Big Boy. A lot of them were animal lovers that were coming together to lend a helping hand if it was needed. My newspaper friend had told me that all hell was going to break loose to rescue Big Boy. Well, he was 100% right! All hell was breaking loose right before my eyes! This is so amazing! My emotions were running wild. There's just no way that this is really happening! Big Boys story in the newspaper wasn't even out yet. It wouldn't hit newsstands for several hours. Yet here were so many people, again I am floored at the power of the internet and social media, and the power of God!

Just sitting back, watching search and rescue get organized was like watching a war movie of Americas finest men and women preparing themselves for a military recon mission. These people had a solid plan, with plans of executing it without failure being an option.

Some people had made signs saying 'We love you Big Boy.' Other people had signs saying 'We're on our way Big Boy.'

A search and rescue team member approached my truck, I rolled down my window. He asked 'Are you Jimmy?' 'Yes', I replied. He then said 'Jimmy there's nothing we need you to do right now. But, here's a shortwave radio so you can help guide us to where you last saw Big Boy. If you could head back up to where you've been going to take food to Big Boy, this would be very helpful to us.'

He was right, there was no more that I could do. This was out of my hands now, watching these professionals do their thing fills me with joy and anticipation as well as peace. Just knowing that Big Boy and his friends are about to be rescued brings me to tears.

I'm not much for being around crowds anyway. Thinking it was time for me to bow out and do what I can do, I left the parking lot. I headed to my familiar parking place along the road, put on my snowshoes and made what I hoped to be, my last hike up this snowy, cold mountain. Here now to do my small part of sitting and watching, listening to this shortwave radio ready to help if need be.

There was no talk on my radio, my anxiety is level high with anticipation as I scan the mountain with my binoculars. Everything is still and quiet, then suddenly 6 snow machines broke over the top of the mountain. They were working their way through the trees, under and over snow covered cliffs. Wow, these people are so skilled on their snow machines! Behind 4 of the snow machines I see 4 large 4–6 foot black sleds that had sides, and what looked to be wide cinch straps. I supposed the straps would be used to secure Big Boy and his friends for their ride back over the mountain to the waiting trailer that would carry them all to food and safety.

The snow machines disappeared from my sight, I couldn't hear their engines anymore. My anxiety level went through the roof.

Then my radio came to life, startling me so bad that I dropped my binoculars. I stood up, my fingers numb from the tight grip that I had kept on the radio in my hand, 'We got him Jimmy! We have Big Boy, and his friends! They are all fine, they are very weak, but I'm sure they're all going to be okay! Whoo hoo! It's a successful rescue Jimmy! They're all loaded up and secured. We're heading back.'

I fell to my knees, dropping the radio. 'Thank you, thank you, thank you' I cried. The tears rolled down my face uncontrollably, falling to the snow where they instantly froze and made the most beautiful crystals that caught the rays of the morning sun, emitting several brilliant rainbows that seemed to dance before me in my blurred but somehow enhanced vision. I reached down in front of me and grasped the beautiful crystals in my hands as I raised my head, the frozen tears clutched tightly in my hands as I watched the 6 snow machines with the 4 black sleds that are now full of strapped down precious cargo. My 4 friends, secured as the snow machines pull them back along the side of the steep ridge and back over the mountain on the same trail that they had come in on.

Chapter 62

I'm in complete awe, there were no words that could explain my feelings at this moment. Tears of gratitude continued to fall for these extraordinary people who had stepped up. Risking their own safety to save this dog that I'd named Big Boy.

Not wanting to go back to the Beaver Mountain parking lot, with who knows how many people would be there by now, I decide to just head home. Big Boy was in the best of care possible. Now all that mattered to me was that my friends were going to be okay.

There was a somber feeling that had taken over my thoughts as I drove off the mountain, thoughts becoming prayer, sending my very best 'thank yous' to first God, and then to every one on the amazing search and rescue team. Thoughts and prayers and my very best 'thank you' going to my friend for going public with Big Boys story. A 'thank you' to my friend for convincing me to make that one phone call that made the rescue possible.

I chuckle to myself as I say to my dogs, who are sleeping, one on the front seat and the other on the backseat, 'Most of the time it's not good when all hell breaks loose, but this time it was such a blessing in disguise.' They both open one eye for a brief moment, my sentence didn't include any words like 'hunting' or 'duck' or 'bird' or any food item, so off into their dreamland they returned to dream about all those things that only a happy dog can dream about.

Chapter 63

Heading home, I'm pretty elated about Big Boy being on his way to safety right now. I'd miss my friend Big Boy. One thing that stands true with true life long friends, is that even if you don't see or speak with each other for long periods of time, your friendship never dissolves. With true life long friends when that time comes when you do see or speak again, it's like nothing has changed between true friends. Everything will always remain exactly the same between us. Sure, there's a lot of things that have changed for one or the other friend, that's just part of life. But real life long friends will always be close, with a genuine caring for each other and their friendship. This is how I feel about my friend Big Boy. There's no doubt in my mind, that as much alike as me and Big Boy are, that he feels exactly the same about me. We are friends for life.

Getting home, there's an empty feeling. Over these last 3 months life had changed, revolving around rescuing Big Boy. It took me some time, a couple of weeks had gone by. I figured that Big Boy was back home and back to being healthy again. There was something that really had me bothered, my gut was still telling me that the owner had been dishonest to not only me, but to everyone else about Big Boy being his dog.

I'd had this picture in my mind, like a snapshot of Big Boy from earlier times when he had watched us on the property next door while we hunted Canadian geese. There was something so unique, so different about Big Boys eyes. His eyes were unlike any other dogs eyes that I had ever seen. Yes, they were a dark brown in color, but there was something else. Something special that made his eyes stand alone, eyes that were spear sharp like they looked straight into your soul. Big Boys eyes were unforgettable. I was sure that I'd seen his eyes before while hunting in the field across from where I suspected Big Boys home was. I had this 'knowing' that Big Boys owner was lying about owning Big Boy to avoid animal abandonment or cruelty charges.

I wanted to see Big Boy again, I needed to know that he was safe. So I made several phone calls. I called fish and game, search and rescue, my friend at the newspaper that had written Big Boys story. No one knew where Big Boy was or who had taken him, or where he was or had gone.

I needed to know the truth about my true friend Big Boy. Deciding to gather up some good treats while taking a truck ride out to where my gut knew that I'd seen Big Boy before. The place where his eyes had made such an impression on me.

Chapter 64

I drove out to the country road that separated two properties. One side was property that was leased by me for hunting Canadian geese, the other side was where in my mind, Big Boy lived. There was no one around, my field was barren with just grain stubble. No geese or any other birds. There were a few cows trying to scoop up any grain kernels that had been left behind. A few hundred yards away, in the other field were about 1,500 sheep. They were just being lazy, most of them appeared to be sleeping. In times that I'd been out there before, there had been 5 Great Pyrenees protecting them.

When doing my search trying to find out where Big Boys home was, a long time before he was rescued, I had come here. I had seen only 4 Great Pyrenees protecting this flock of sheep. If there were 5 Great Pyrenees now, it would be almost 100% confirmation of my gut feeling. Seeing him and his eyes would leave absolutely no doubt.

I pulled over to the side of the road and stopped my truck. Reaching for my binoculars, I scanned the field of sheep. Counting first 1, then 2 then 3, then over in a corner by himself was number 4. I'm not seeing a number 5. I'm thinking that being wrong would be fine with me. Maybe my mind and my gut had wrongly accused this rancher of lying about being the owner of Big Boy.

But I feel his presence in me here, just like I had many times before up on the mountain. Big Boy is here.

I have to know for sure, so I decided to get out of my truck and stand up on the top of the toolbox in the back of my truck to get a better view. Maybe Big Boy was laying down, or maybe he just isn't here. I thoroughly scanned over the field and flock several times. Not seeing Big Boy, I got back into my truck, turned around and started heading towards home.

I came around the far corner of the field where another road intersected, as I turn my eyes look into the field and there stands Big Boy. It's him! He IS here! I stopped my truck in the middle of the road and I get out, my truck running and the door open wide, my eyes filling with tears as I run over to the fence. 'Here Big Boy, here Big Boy, there's my friend Big Boy!' Woooooof wooooof wooooof, bark bark, bark. Here he comes, running full blast towards me, his strides were long, woooooof wooooooof wooooooof. His powerful body just glided forward towards me woooooof wooooooof wooooooof. 'Hi Big Boy! How are you my friend? You made it home!' Big Boy was waddling side to side, his tail making large circles behind him, his tongue out, ears flapping, he was happy to see me.

'Hi Big Boy look what I brought you,' Big Boys instincts remained strong, he stayed a short distance from me. I wanted to go through the fence and just grab him and give him a big bear hug, but instead I settled for his greeting. Big Boy was so excited that he was twisting in circles, doing funny jumps, he rolled around while making funny noises. 'Big Boy are you showing off? Big Boy you're a big galoot. Come over here my friend, I've got treats for you.' His excitement I determined wasn't showing off, I believe that he was letting me know that he was okay and happy to be home.

Big Boy came within about 2 feet of me. Throwing his snacks towards him, he grabbed them up and ate them all. I'd sure love to take you home with me Big Boy, but I know you're happy here doing your job, protecting your friends for the rest of your life. I'll have to bring you some corn dogs next time my friend!

Big Boy sat down, our eyes met. Our eyes communicated a language between us that can't be spoken with words. It's a language that only our hearts can understand. It's a language that only lifetime true friends have an ability to communicate through.

Epilogue

Big Boy and I stayed true friends for 5 more years. I'd come and visit him from time to time in the winter months when he was home on vacation, bringing him good treats (once in awhile corn dogs!). He always greeted me with sheer joy. Big Boy passed away from natural causes. I will never forget my life long true friend, and our adventure together. We had a bond that held strong until the very last day.

I especially will never forget how God revealed Himself to me through this experience. How He used a very special dog to teach me to let go of my pride, and to place my trust in Him.

And how I need to remember to count my lucky stars.

Printed in the United States
By Bookmasters